THE LAND
OF THE
BIBLE

Edited by

JAMES I. PACKER, A.M., D.PHIL.

Regent College

MERRILL C. TENNEY, A.M., Ph.D.

Wheaton Graduate School

WILLIAM WHITE, JR., Th.M., Ph.D.

THOMAS NELSON PUBLISHERS
Nashville • Camden • New York

Published in Nashville, Tennessee, by Thomas Nelson, Inc., Publishers and distributed in Canada by Lawson Falle, Ltd., Cambridge, Ontario.

Printed in the United States of America.

Library of Congress Cataloging in Publication Data

The Land of the Bible.

  Includes bibliographical references and index.
  1. Bible—Geography. 2. Palestine—Historical
geography. 3. Nature in the Bible. 4. Animals in the
Bible. 5. Plants in the Bible. I. Packer, J. I. (James
Innell) II. Tenney, Merrill Chapin, 1904-
III. White, William, 1934-
BS621.L3   1985   220.9'1   85-5039
ISBN 0-8407-5983-5

INTRODUCTION

The fertile crescent, the land of the Bible, just how fertile was it? Abraham, the father of the faithful, saw it as very fertile. He traveled its entire length, all the way from Ur of the Mesopotamian valley through the highlands of Haran, down the great rift—a sink of which holds the Dead Sea—across the sands of Sinai into the green belt of Egypt. This area of the land was livable, even lush, because of the ever-recurring floods of the Nile. Then he accepted God's promise that his descendants would inherit Canaan, a land of milk and honey.

Today's traveler often has trouble seeing Palestine as a fertile land. What makes this dry, barren country a land flowing with milk and honey?

Was the land so different then? It was; yet it was also the same. Not everything has remained the same, but some has. Not everything has changed, but some things have. The land's occupants have caused changes. They overgrazed the land, cultivated foolishly, carved roads, and built towns. The winds and the rains have also brought change. This book, *The Land of the Bible,* takes the land as it is but describes it as it was for those who once lived there—the people to whom God spoke and through whom even now He speaks to us.

Do you have questions about the land? About its animal life? About its resources? Questions like, Why was it called a land of milk and honey? How could grapes grow so large as those brought to Kadesh-Barnea from Eschol? How could the slime mentioned in Genesis 14:10 be used for mortar? What makes the Dead Sea? Why is it salty? Why doesn't it grow larger? Or does it? *The Land of the Bible* gives answers to such questions and many others which you have always asked about the geography, animals, plants, minerals and gems, and agriculture of the land of Palestine.

What about the unicorn of Job 39:9? What is an ossifrage, spoken of in Leviticus 11:13? What kind of fish swallowed Jonah? Exactly what was the gopher wood which Noah used to build the ark?

The Land of the Bible gives answers and creates understanding about scores of interesting questions just like these.

What did the people of Bible times eat? Wheat? Barley? Millet? Corn? Vegetables? Nuts? Was the corn the same as Indian maize? You will find answers in *The Land of the Bible*—a handbook to the land of Palestine and its creatures and to the people to whom God entrusted the Promised Land. As a student of the Bible, read it and use it in order to understand God's Word more fully.

TABLE OF CONTENTS

1

THE GEOGRAPHY OF PALESTINE

Palestine is the heartland of three major religions of the world. Judaism, Christianity, and Islam each trace their beginnings to this small tract of land. Here God revealed Himself to the patriarchs and prophets, to Jesus and His apostles.

Studying the geography of Palestine is not a recent pursuit. Early church fathers such as Jerome felt it was important for an understanding of the Bible.

Many Christians no longer depend on maps and globes to show them the face of Palestine. They can see the ancient sites with their own eyes. Place names leap to life as they walk the ground where biblical cities once stood. Scripture takes on new reality when they step into the Holy Land.

Palestine is a magnificent country rich in history, a land of contrasts. Modern and ancient ways of life go on side by side. Barren deserts clash with the lush foliage of oases.

THE GREAT RIFT VALLEY

What can compare with the beauty of the Jordan River Valley? Barren slopes of the Judean wilderness loom over the curves of the Jordan River. But since the 1967 cease-fire, this river has marked the boundary between the modern states of Israel and Jordan. Unfortunately, it is now dangerous even to approach the Jordan.

Impressive though it is, the Jordan Valley is only a small part of the Great Rift Valley, which stretches from Syria to Africa. South of the Jordan Valley and Arabah wilderness, the Red Sea covers over 2,200 km. (1,400 mi.) of the Great Rift Valley's floor. The

Red Sea extends to the Indian Ocean; its waters lap against East Africa on one side and the Arabian Peninsula on the other. In Central Africa, the Great Rift Valley cradles the Rudolf, Albert, Victoria, Tanganyika, and Nyasa Lakes.

Thousands of years ago, immense pressures beneath the earth's surface created the Great Rift Valley. As the earth cracked in the upheaval, parts of the earth's crust were pushed up. Thus mountains follow the valley for its full length on both sides.

A. The Surrounding Land. In northern Palestine, the Lebanon and Hermon mountain ranges flank the valley. During certain months of the year these mountains cool the moisture-filled clouds causing heavy rainfall, and in winter they collect snow. Springs and runoff waters create streams that flow into the Sea of Galilee to the south and are eventually channeled out into the Jordan River.

The Jordan meanders southward from the Sea of Galilee through the valley, finally bringing its waters into the Dead Sea. Here the water is trapped; it cannot escape except by evaporation because at the south end of the Sea the ground rises.

The higher ground becomes the Arabah wilderness, which reaches from the Dead Sea south to the Gulf of Eilat on the Red Sea. On the east are the sharp mountains of Edom; to the west are the Negev Desert and the Mediterranean Sea.

Biblical authors introduce us to the geographical divisions of Palestine. Moses told the people of Israel, "Turn you, and take your journey, and go to the mount of the Amorites, and unto all the places nigh thereunto, in the plain, in the hills, and in the vale, and in the south, and by the sea side, to the land of the Canaanites, and unto Lebanon, unto the great river, the river Euphrates" (Deut. 1:7). Later we are told that "Joshua smote all the country of the hills, and of the south, and of the vale, and of the springs, and all their kings" (Josh. 10:40).

B. Earthquakes. The subterranean forces that formed the Great Rift Valley are still at work. Even today the land rests uneasily, at the mercy of tremors caused by shifts of the great blocks of land that form the earth's crust. Through the centuries tremors and quakes have shaken the valley.

The Bible mentions some of these earthquakes. Such a forceful quake shook Palestine during King Uzziah's reign that the prophet Amos dated a message by it: "Two years before the earthquake"

(Amos 1:1). Zechariah referred to it 270 years later: "Ye shall flee, like as ye fled from before the earthquake in the days of Uzziah king of Judah" (Zech. 14:5).

Another earthquake took place about five hundred years later. It occurred at the moment Jesus died on the cross: "And the earth did quake, and the rocks rent; And the graves were opened" (Matt. 27:51–52).

Poets and prophets saw earthquakes as instruments of God's judgment: "Thou shalt be visited of the LORD of Hosts with thunder, and with earthquake, and great noise, with storm and tempest, and the flame of devouring fire" (Isa. 29:6). And "Then the earth shook and trembled; the foundations also of the hills moved and were shaken, because he was wroth" (Psa. 18:7).

Genesis 19:24-28 reports the destruction of Sodom and Gomorrah by "brimstone and fire." Some believe this was a divinely-

Palestine. This aerial photograph taken in 1930 shows the western edge of the Jordan Valley in the foreground. The houses and roads of modern Jericho lie in the center of the picture, and a white arrow indicates the dark oval mound of the Tell es-Sultan (biblical Jericho). To the left, behind the mountains, lies the desert of Judah. In the distance is the Mediterranean Sea. Although the picture was probably retouched (due to technical imperfections of aerial photography when it was taken), it gives a striking impression of the Palestinean highlands.

ordered earthquake that released a cloud of natural gas, which exploded. Located in the southern part of the Jordan Valley, the ruins of these cities were gradually covered with the water of the Dead Sea, to remove any trace of the wickedness practiced in them.

Ancient sources mention other earthquakes. Archaeologists have unearthed the results of their devastation in Jericho, Qumran, Hazor, and elsewhere.

THE FERTILE CRESCENT

God promised the land of Canaan to Abraham and his descendants. It is a fertile country, bounded by deserts to the east and south and shaken by an occasional earthquake.

Canaan is the southern tip of the area known as the Fertile Crescent. Unlike the terrain around it, this narrow semicircle of land in the Near East receives enough moisture to grow crops. The green horseshoe starts at the Persian Gulf on the eastern end and extends to the southern part of Canaan on the western end. It is bordered by the Mediterranean Sea on the west, mountains to the north, and desert regions to the south and east. From this well-favored strip of land rose the great nations of the Old Testament.

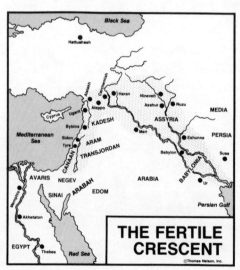

A. Palestine: A Strategic Location. God chose a prominent place for His people to prove themselves to be a "holy nation." The land of Canaan was strategically located between the great civilizations of the Near East. Egypt lay to the southwest, Phoenicia and Aram (Syria) to the north, and Assyria and Babylonia to the east. Unlike Egypt, Canaan could not isolate herself from her neighbors.

In fact, the inhabitants of Canaan were *forced* to get involved in world politics. In times of war they were never safe. Canaan was the land-bridge over which Egypt passed on her way to the north. Assyrians, Babylonians, and Greeks also trampled Canaan when they headed south in their conquest of the Near East.

Yet there were advantages to being crisscrossed by surrounding cultures. Canaan was enriched by the art and literature of other nations, as well as by their building techniques and scientific accomplishments. In the teeming center of the ancient Near East, God called His people in Canaan to be a challenge to the nations.

"A goodly heritage of the hosts of nations" (Jer. 3:19)—so did the prophet Jeremiah describe Palestine, the Promised Land. It is a pleasant land, this southwestern branch of the Fertile Crescent. In contrast to the sea, mountains, and deserts that enclose it, Palestine offers fertile soil, water, and a pleasant climate. These favorable conditions enticed early man to settle there. Indeed, whole civilizations rose and fell on the soil of Palestine before Israel claimed it as her own.

B. The Canaanites. By the time Abraham came into the land, Canaan had long been inhabited. The first settlers dwelled in caves in the Mount Carmel region. They lived by hunting wild game and collecting wild grains, vegetables, and fruits. Gradually they moved to small villages and planted fields of wheat, barley, and legumes. Herds and flocks further expanded their diet. As the villagers produced more than they could use, they began trading. The small communities then developed road systems for traders to move from village to village with their wares of produce, textiles, pottery, and jewelry.

Jericho is a good example of such developments. This well-watered region is a beautiful oasis in the desert north of the Dead Sea and several miles west of the Jordan River. Archaeologists have found few signs of the early stages of the city's growth. They surmise that the people lived in flimsy tents and huts. At first the people of Jericho were semi-nomadic, moving from place to place in search of food. But with the development of the flint, sickle, and primitive plow, they could support themselves off a smaller parcel of land. They built houses and the population increased, and gradually the village became a city. To protect against destruction by jealous neighbors or passing enemies, they erected a wall around the settlement. When Abraham arrived in Canaan, Jericho had already passed through several cycles of building, destruction, and rebuilding.

THE PROMISED LAND

Even in twentieth-century ears, those words create excitement. From the very first book of the Bible, God's promise of the land to Abraham emerges as a theme again and again.

A. Abraham's Journey. Genesis 11:31–12:10 describes the incredible journey that Abraham made in search of the land of promise. From the Persian Gulf he traveled the full length of the Fertile Crescent, even going as far as Egypt.

In 1866, archaeologists positively identified a site in southern Iraq as Ur, the place of Abraham's birth (Gen. 11:28). The city was located on the Euphrates River, and in ancient times it was an important commercial center. It prospered for thousands of years, up to the fourth century B.C. Excavations at Ur have unearthed a ziggurat (a three-staged step tower) dedicated to the moon god, Nanna.

Abraham's father, Terah, led the family's migration from Ur. Abraham, his brother Nahor, and his nephew Lot took their families, servants, and possessions on the long trek. They journeyed over 1,100 km. (700 mi.) to Haran, another thriving city on one of

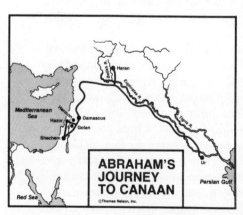

ABRAHAM'S JOURNEY TO CANAAN

the trade routes from Assyria to the Mediterranean Sea. Haran was located at the Balikh River, a northern tributary of the Euphrates. The people here also worshiped the moon god.

Abraham was 75 when God told him: "Get thee out of thy country, and from thy kindred, and from thy father's house, unto a land that I will shew thee"

(Gen. 12:1). He left Haran, taking his wife Sarai and nephew Lot, and their possessions. They took a road leading through Syria to Damascus.

After that point, it is interesting to speculate on the routes Abraham might have taken to Canaan. From Damascus one road led past the Hermon Mountain range and over the Golan Heights to the Hula Valley. The Hula Lake was a swampy reservoir of water from the melting snow of Mount Hermon, runoff rain water, and springs at the foot of the mountain ranges. South of the lake, the water ran through a narrow canal to the Sea of Galilee. Caravans crossed the narrow canal at a ford. From there the road passed by Hazor and the Sea of Galilee to Megiddo, then through the valley of Dothan to Shechem.

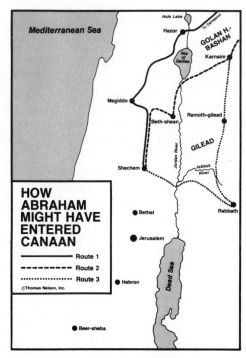

HOW ABRAHAM MIGHT HAVE ENTERED CANAAN

——— Route 1
– – – – Route 2
· · · · · · Route 3

©Thomas Nelson, Inc.

Or Abraham's caravan may have used the Bashan Road, which leads through the Golan Heights (Bashan). At the eastern edge of the Yarmuk gorge, the road turns westward and gradually descends to the Jordan Valley. There the Sea of Galilee, the Jordan River, and the Yarmuk come together. Once in the Jordan Valley, a traveler can quickly go to Beth-shean and from there to Shechem through the valleys of Jezreel and Dothan. This route was not traveled as frequently as the Hula Valley road. The trail from the Golan Heights to the Jordan Valley descended sharply, and part of the way it followed secondary roads less fit for large caravans or troops.

A third route that Abraham may have taken was probably used by Jacob when he deserted Laban in Haran. It led directly south, passing by the cities of Karnaim and Ashtaroth, and between Irbid

7

and Ramoth-gilead. Ten miles before Rabbath-bene-ammon (the present city of Amman, capital of Jordan), it veered slightly north and due west toward the Jordan Valley. The road descended to the gorge of the Jabbok River, crossed it at the ford of Mahanaim, then turned southward to Adam, where it could cross the Jordan River. From there to Shechem, the road leading out of the valley followed a rather steep incline by the Wadi Far'a for nearly 32 km. (20 mi.).

We know Abraham came through Shechem. It was a major intersection, controlling traffic going every direction. Archaeologists believe that Shechem was not a fortified city until the time of Jacob (about 1900 B.C.). But it was strategically located at a pass between Mount Ebal on the north and Mount Gerizim on the south. The road from Wadi Far'a came into the Tirzah-Shechem road, which south of Shechem was called "the plain of Meonenim" (Judg. 9:37), or "the direction of the Diviners' Oak" (in the RSV). At Shechem a road turned off toward the Mediterranean, connecting Shechem with the major highway of Palestine, the Via Maris (Latin, "Way of the Sea").

At Shechem, the Lord promised to give the land to Abraham's descendants (Gen. 12:7). As a memorial of the promise, Abraham built an altar on the plain of Moreh (Gen. 12:6). God did not give Abraham exact boundaries, but He later assured the patriarch that the land on all four sides would be granted to his descendants (Gen. 13:14-15).

God's covenant with Abraham stated the promise even more clearly: "Unto thy seed have I given this land, from the river of

Jericho. The oldest city in Palestine, Jericho was attacked and conquered by Joshua during the Israelites' conquest of Canaan. The city lies 16 km. (10 mi.) northwest of where the Jordan River enters the Dead Sea, and about 27 km. (17 mi.) northeast of Jerusalem. The mountains of Judea rise abruptly from the plains just west of the city.

Egypt unto the great river, the river Euphrates" (Gen. 15:18). The promise was confirmed to Isaac (Gen. 26:3) and to Jacob (Gen. 28:13).

B. Land of the Patriarchs. God revealed to the patriarchs the lines of Israel's conquest. Biblical history continued to revolve around the cities, regions, and shrines where the patriarchs lived and worshiped. God commanded Abraham, "Arise, walk through the land in the length of it and in the breadth of it; for I will give it unto thee" (Gen. 13:17). Until they could gain control of Canaan, the patriarchs obeyed that command and took the land in faith for their descendants.

The patriarchal family was forced to leave Shechem after Jacob's sons Simeon and Levi rashly killed all the males of the city. Jacob rebuked them: "Ye have troubled me to make me to stink among the inhabitants of the land,...and I being few in number, they shall gather themselves together against me, and slay me; and I shall be destroyed, I and my house" (Gen. 34:30). God sent them to Bethel, where Jacob built another altar. To prepare for that holy experience, Jacob's household buried all their foreign gods by an oak tree and purified themselves. They took the Way of the Diviners' Oak to Bethel, where God had revealed Himself in Jacob's dream of the ladder twenty years earlier (Gen. 28). Again at Bethel, God reassured Jacob that his descendants would occupy the land (Gen. 35:12).

Bethel and Shechem were not the only places where the patriarchs lived and built altars. Their footsteps led to Hebron and as far south as Beer-sheba in the Negev Desert. They canvassed the area that Joshua would later conquer.

Indeed, the patriarchs laid the groundwork for both good and ill for their descendants in the land of Canaan. Abraham's and Isaac's involvement with the king of Gerar in the Philistine plain (Gen. 20:1-18; 26:17-22) foreshadowed future conflicts, when the Philistines would press hard against the Israelites in the hill country. But many sacred sites of the Israelites in this period became important cities. Jerusalem, where the priest-king Melchizedek blessed Abraham, became the royal residence of King David and the very center of the Jewish religion after Solomon built the temple there.

Jacob's son Joseph brought the Israelites into Egypt. They entered Egypt as the *people* (clan) of Israel (Jacob); but there God forged them into a *nation*. The Egyptians felt threatened by the "population explosion" of the Israelites. To thwart their growing power, the Egyptians forced them to serve as slaves in the land of Goshen. Yet at the appointed time, God promised them: "And I will bring you in unto the land,...I did swear to give...to Abraham, to Isaac, and to Jacob; and I will give it you for an heritage; I am the LORD" (Exod. 6:8). God sent Moses to lead the people "Up out of the affliction of Egypt unto...a land flowing with milk and honey" (Exod. 3:17).

God planned that His people would enter the Promised Land and become a nation unlike the surrounding nations. They would show their faith in God by grateful obedience. Keeping God's commandments would ensure their success: "Hear therefore, O Israel, and observe to do it; that it may be well with thee, and that ye may increase mightily" (Deut. 6:3).

God chose the Israelites to be His witnesses in the Promised Land. They could demonstrate the faith of the patriarchs, who had successfully dealt with the nations around them. God's chosen people would grace the chosen land. This was God's third promise to Abraham, that through him and his descendants the nations would be blessed (Gen. 12:3).

Israel's possibilities within the Promised Land—its very future—depended on two things: its responsible use of the land and its faithful obedience to the terms of the Covenant. God looked for the day when Israel's observance of His laws would cause the nations to declare: "Surely this great nation is a wise and understanding people" (Deut. 4:6).

C. Extent of the Promised Land. We don't know the exact boundaries of the Promised Land. God revealed to Abraham that he and his descendants would receive the land of Canaan, but He originally promised them a much larger area than that. When Lot's and Abraham's shepherds quarreled over the land, Abraham wisely offered to give his nephew Lot first choice of the territory. Lot decided to settle in the well-watered Jordan Valley in the east. God then told Abraham: "Lift up now thine eyes, and look from the place where thou art northward, and southward, and eastward, and westward: For all the land which thou seest, to thee will I give it, and to thy seed for ever" (Gen. 13:14-15). The boundary lines

The Dead Sea. The lowest body of water in the world, the Dead Sea is about 390 m. (1,300 ft.) below sea level. Its depth is estimated at another 91 m. (300 ft.). Located in southern Palestine, the Dead Sea is 80 km. (50 mi.) long and not more than 18 km. (11 mi.) at its widest point. The sea has no outlet. It is so filled with salts and other minerals that fish brought down by the Jordan River are killed within a few moments. The Dead Sea is referred to as the "Salt Sea" in the Old Testament (cf. Gen. 14:3).

were not settled, though Abraham's territory obviously ended where Lot's flocks grazed.

God made the "land of promise" a part of His covenant with Abraham. Abraham "believed the LORD and he counted it to him for righteousness" (Gen. 15:6). In return, God solemnly promised to give to his descendants the land "from the river of Egypt unto the great river, the river Euphrates" (Gen. 15:18).

Several hundred years later, when Moses reminded the Israelites of that promise, he described the boundaries of the Promised Land: the Arabah, the mountainous regions, and Shephelah, and the Negev and the coastal plains by the Mediterranean Sea, from the southern border of Canaan through Lebanon up to the Euphrates (Deut. 1:7).

By this time the Israelites already lived in the Transjordan. God allowed the tribes of Reuben and Gad, as well as part of the tribe of Manasseh, to settle in the newly-occupied land of the Amorites east of the Jordan (Num. 21:21–35:32). This territory extended the borders of the Promised Land even farther. But Moses still did not set a definite eastern boundary.

God ordered Joshua to take all the territory specified by Moses: "From the wilderness and this Lebanon even unto the great river, the river Euphrates, all the land of the Hittites, and unto the Great Sea toward the going down of the sun, shall be your coast" (Josh. 1:4). However, during the conquest of Canaan the people of Israel failed to take the total area promised them, partly because they were unfaithful to God. God punished the Israelites by holding them back from complete victory. "I sware in my wrath that they should not enter into my rest" (Psa. 95:11). Each tribe lacked part of its inheritance.

D. Efforts to Expand. During the period of the judges, Israel tried unsuccessfully to enlarge its tribal territories. Even Saul, the first king, was not powerful enough to drive out or subdue the other nations.

Yet God allowed Saul's successor, King David, to control the land of promise except for "the land of the Hittites" (cf. Josh. 1:4). David was a man "after God's heart." Because he honored God in his military pursuits, God granted him victory over the Ammonites, Moabites, and Edomites in the east, over the Philistines in the west, and over the marauding nomadic bands in the south. In fact, his conquests reached almost to the Euphrates River, as far north as Hammath (2 Sam. 8).

Solomon inherited the kingdom at its peak. "For he had dominion over all the region on this side the river, from Tiphsah even to Azzah, over all the kings on this side the river: and he had peace on all sides round about him" (1 Kings 4:24). But from the latter part of Solomon's reign, the nation of Israel went steadily downhill. First the kingdom was divided into two nations—Israel and

Land of Ephraim. The prophet Hosea predicted that God would punish the tribe of Ephraim, which lived in these fertile hills north of Jerusalem (cf. Hosea 12—13). Hosea said, "Now they sin more and more, and have made them...idols according to their own understanding..." (Hosea 13:2).

Judah. Wars racked both of these kingdoms until their enemies forced them out of the land.

E. Fertility of the Land. A tourist to Palestine from the fertile plains of America might wonder if Moses was in his right mind when he described the Promised Land as "a good land, a land of brooks of water, of fountains and depths that spring out of the valleys and hills; A land of wheat, and barley, and vines, and fig trees, and pomegranates; a land of oil olive, and honey; A land wherein thou shalt eat bread without scarceness, thou shalt not lack any thing in it" (Deut. 8:7-9). But Moses addressed those words to a people who had just spent 40 years in the desert! The earliest American pioneers, crossing the desert into the coastal plain areas of California, might have found similar soil conditions and geographical contrasts. The Promised Land held boundless possibilities in contrast to the harsh, dry regions of the Sinai, Negev, and Arabah.

However, the Promised Land was no Garden of Eden. The Israelites may have envisioned endless valleys of crops and hillsides adorned with grasses, herbs, and flowers; but that is not what they found. Thorns and thistles cover the rocky land. During summer months a dull reddish-brown color on the slopes indicates parched vegetation. Nevertheless, the land is highly fertile compared to the surrounding deserts.

The Promised Land offered good opportunities for making a living with its water and tillable soil. But the Israelites discovered that it was not easy to take advantage of those opportunities. They had to tame the land. The Israelite farmer had to deal with rocks, thorns, thistles. He feared the sun, which scorched young seedlings that were not rooted deeply enough to draw water from a depth. He learned dependence on the Lord, "for he maketh his sun to rise on the evil and on the good, and sendeth rain on the just and on the unjust" (Matt. 5:45).

Jesus illustrated the farmer's plight with His parable of the sower. The sower spread the seed all over the field, but only the seed which fell on "good ground" produced a crop. The remaining seed fell on rocks and among thistles and soon died (Matt. 13:3-8).

What the Israelites could accomplish with the soil of Palestine depended entirely on their relationship with the Lord. He promised to bless them materially for their obedience: "The LORD shall open unto thee his good treasure, the heaven to give the rain unto thy land in his season, and to bless all the work of thine hand" (Deut. 28:12). Disobedience, however, would bring material judgment: "But...if thou wilt not hearken unto the voice of the LORD thy God...thy heaven that is over thy head shall be brass, and the earth that is under thee shall be iron. The LORD shall make the rain of thy land powder and dust" (Deut. 28:15a, 23, 24). "Thou shalt carry much seed out into the field, and shalt gather but little in; for the locust shall consume it. Thou shalt plant the vineyards, and dress them, but shalt neither drink of the wine, nor gather the grapes; for the worms shall eat them" (Deut. 28:38-39). If the Israelites did not heed the Lord, they would lose the very land God promised to them: "Ye shall be plucked from off the land whither thou goest to possess it" (Deut. 28:63b). Sadly, that very thing happened.

1. Soil. When Israel first occupied the land, they lived in the hill country near the central mountain range of Canaan. The Israelite farmers had to learn how to eke out an existence from the hills, which were largely composed of limestone rock. Though limestone weathers into soil very slowly, it is very fertile.

Rains easily wash the rich hillside soil down streams to low-lying valleys. To prevent erosion, farmers planted fruit trees and vines or built terraces.

Terraces abounded in the hill country. Sometimes a layer of rock resisted weathering and formed a natural wall. This held in place the reddish soil that the farmer could plant with wheat, barley, legumes, and vegetables, in addition to fruit trees and vines. When there was no natural wall, the farmer had to clear the area of ever-present stones and use them to build a wall at the lower side of the hill.

Vineyards also abounded in Palestine, and biblical authors often mentioned them symbolically, as Isaiah did: "My well-beloved hath a vineyard in a very fruitful hill: and he fenced it, and gathered out the stones thereof, and planted it with the choicest vines" (Isa. 5:1-2). In this passage, God is the owner of the vineyard Israel. The work of preparing the vineyard represents God's love and care for Israel, who nonetheless failed to produce the harvest of righteousness He desired.

2. Precipitation. Have you ever wondered what the Bible means by "former rains" and "latter rains"? Farmers in Palestine counted on the "former rains" of fall, which permitted seeds to

---

Hula Basin Project

Hula Lake no longer exists. Where gentle waters once shimmered in the shadow of Mount Hermon, farmers now cultivate an "agricultural paradise." In draining this lake and its papyrus marshes, the modern Israelis reclaimed about 45,000 acres of rich peat soil, enough farming land to support 100,000 people.

For the tiny nation of Israel, both water and land are in short supply. After the State of Israel was established, waves of immigrants landed upon the shores of the Promised Land. Though Israel welcomed the newcomers, it agonized over the lack of space available for settlement. Clearly the government had to make the best possible use of the land it had.

The new nation immediately adopted a far-reaching policy of land and water use. Officials began a comprehensive inventory of the land. All waters—surface, subterranean, even sewage—were declared public property and put under governmental control. At Israel's request, the Food and Agricultural Organization of the United Nations sent a team to help develop a soil and water conservation program, and to determine the best use of all available resources.

The Hula Basin Project was Israel's first major reclamation program. Waters converged in Hula Lake to form the nation's water lifeline, the Jordan River. In Roman times and earlier, the Hula Basin was fertile and populated. But by the twentieth century, it consisted primarily of 90 sq. km. (44 sq. mi.) of swamps. The area was a public menace. Its humid marshlands bred malaria and blackwater fever; they also made a fine hiding place for enemy infiltrators. Worst of all, the water there was being *wasted*. Wildlife inhabited the area, but the water was of no use to

the people of Israel.

Reclaiming the marshes of Hula Lake was not a new idea. During the Ottoman Empire (A.D. 1300–1500), Syrians got permission from their Turkish overlords for a similar project, but never followed through. In 1869, a Scottish adventurer named John MacGregor explored the area via canoe. He suggested that someone should cut a hole at the bottom end of the lake and drain it. Three generations later (1951–1957), Israel did.

Workmen began by blasting a hole in the basalt rock that dammed the southern end of the lake. This widened and deepened the mouth of the lake, and lowered the water level. With a temporary partition holding back the water, giant dredges dug channels through the swamps. When the partition was removed, the water flowed through 46 km. (29 mi.) of drainage canals.

Israel's gains are many. The peat deposits of the former lake bed have been called the finest soil in Israel. Grapes, sugar cane, cotton, vegetables, grains, and fruits are grown on the valley floor. The first yield was three times as great as anticipated.

A 750-acre plot was preserved for a wildlife refuge. In this natural aviary, more than 450 species of birds have been sighted. Pelicans soon discovered that fish were still available, lake or no lake. This posed a serious problem for certain Israeli entrepreneurs, who built ponds in the Hula district to raise fish commercially.

Water still flows into Hula Basin from the slopes and springs of Mount Hermon. But that water now serves Israel. Some stays in the valley to irrigate local crops; conservationists say that enough water is saved to irrigate 17,000 to 25,000 acres.

germinate and seedlings to develop into strong plants. Equally essential were the "latter rains" of February and March, which enabled plants to mature in the following months. October to April is considered the winter season and is cold and rainy.

In Palestine, summer's warm air makes rain unlikely. Rain is also rare in May and September. Weather varies in the transition months between spring and summer (April to mid-June) and between summer and fall (September and October). The onset of cold weather may trigger heavy showers and endanger ripening crops: "As snow in summer, and as rain in harvest, so honor is not seemly for a fool" (Prov. 26:1).

To the prophets, the rain signaled God's continued blessing and favor upon his children: "Be glad then, ye children of Zion, and rejoice in the LORD your God: for he hath given you the former rain moderately, and he will cause to come down for you the rain, the former rain, and the latter rain in the first month" (Joel 2:23).

Hosea likened God's presence to the refreshing spring rain: "He shall come unto us as the rain, as the latter and former rain unto the earth" (Hos. 6:3b).

THE
PROMISED
LAND
© Thomas Nelson, Inc.

Lack of rain spelled failure for the farmer. As we have seen, God made His gift of rain depend on His people's continued faithfulness (Deut. 11:13-14).

Israel's unfaithfulness brought many seasons of drought. Naomi and her family left Bethlehem for the fields of Moab because of drought (Ruth 1:1). Elijah prayed that no rain or dew would fall for three years so that the people of Israel, seeing God's judgment on them, might return to Him (1 Kings 17:1;

Amos 4:7). Drought often led to famine, a condition frequently mentioned in the Bible (Luke 15:14).

The rainfall in Palestine varies widely from place to place. At one extreme, the southern Negev receives 5 cm. (2 in.) per year, while Mount Hermon may be drenched with 152 cm. (60 in.) of precipitation.

Palestine's rainfall is directly related to the latitude and height of the land. The mountainous regions receive the most—from 61 to 91 cm. (24 to 36 in.) in northern Galilee and from 51 to 71 cm. (20 to 28 in.) in Samaria and Judah. South of the line between Gaza and En-gedi a mere 31 cm. (12 in.) of rain falls; south of Beer-sheba, only 20 cm. (8 in.). The rain also decreases from west to east. Perhaps 20" falls on the coast at Tel Aviv, or at Jerusalem, but only 10 to 20 cm. (4 to 8 in.) falls a few miles to the east at Jericho and the Jordan River.

An estimated 60 to 70 percent of the precipitation is lost through evaporation because of the land's high temperatures and low humidity. Only 10 to 25 percent is absorbed for agricultural purposes.

So the dew that falls approximately 250 nights of the year is very essential. Some vegetation depends entirely on the dew's moisture. We understand why Elijah included dew in his prophecy to Ahab: "There shall not be dew nor rain these years, but according to my word" (1 Kings 17:1b). It is an exhilarating experience to wake up in the Negev desert on a summer morning and see a thick fog! A visitor to this region can appreciate why the Psalmist said: "Behold, how good and pleasant it is for brethren to dwell together in unity! It is like the...dew of Hermon, and as the dew that descended upon mountains of Zion" (Psa. 133:1, 3). Yet the dew evaporates quickly and it became proverbial to compare Israel's faithlessness to dew (cf. Hos. 6:4).

Palestine also gets snow. The majestic snow of Mount Hermon can be seen from a great distance until midsummer. Jeremiah referred to the snowy mountains when he flailed Israel's faithless ways: "Does the snow of Lebanon leave the crags of Sirion? Do the mountain waters run dry, the cold flowing streams? But my people have forgotten me" (Jer. 18:14-15a, RSV).

The hill country of Judah averages two days of snow, which melts rapidly when the daytime temperature rises. However, a blizzard hit Palestine in 1950, bringing 69 cm. (27 in.) of snow to Jerusalem and 53 cm. (21 in.) to Acre!

3. Winds. Wind is both a boon and a bane to Palestine. Her hot climate is eased by cool Mediterranean winds during the day. Chill evenings provide a welcome change from the day's heat in desert and hill country. The moisture-laden seawinds combine with cool air at night to give Palestine her vital dew.

A southeasterly wind marks the change of seasons in Palestine, from spring to summer and from summer to fall. Jeremiah 4:11 mentions "a hot wind from the bare heights in the desert." This dry wind loaded with dust makes the people very uncomfortable.

The Bible's "east wind" may be what the Arabs call a *khamsin*. The *khamsin* leaves people irritable and they feel like doing nothing, because of the oppressive heat. "When the sun did arise, God prepared a vehement east wind; and the sun beat upon the head of Jonah, that he fainted, and wished in himself to die, and said, It is better for me to die than to live" (Jon. 4:8).

The land of Israel may be divided into 6 regions. The Jordan Valley runs down the center of Palestine:

The *Upper Jordan* extends from the Lebanon Mountains to the Sea of Galilee. The area that is usually called the *Jordan Valley* lies between the Sea of Galilee and the Dead Sea.

Galilee is the northernmost area of Palestine between the Jordan River and the Mediterranean coast. *Samaria* spreads between these natural boundaries in central Palestine, while *Judah* does so in the extreme south.

Transjordan is all the land east of the Jordan River, east and south of the Dead Sea. Its eastern border is the Syrian Desert.

THE JORDAN VALLEY

The Jordan River courses through the center of Palestine. It has also been the center of Israel's social and economic life, both in ancient times and today.

A. The Upper Jordan. God first gave the coastal plains to the tribe of Dan for their inheritance. However, as the Philistines grew in power the Danites couldn't hold the land, and they moved to the

Upper Jordan Valley, far from the political centers of Jerusalem and Samaria (Judg. 18). They never fully used the 26 sq. km. (11 sq. mi.) of the valley, as it held many streams, swamps, and small lakes. Mountains hedge the valley on three sides: the Naphtali Range to the west, the Hermon Range to the north, and the Golan Heights (Bashan) to the east.

The encircling mountains, drawing abundant rain and snow, give this region the highest precipitation in Israel, 7 to 15 cm. (3 to 6 in.) annually. Runoff water and melting snow flow underground into springs to provide a year-round supply of fresh water.

1. Mount Hermon. The Danites settled in the fruitful valley at the foot of majestic Mount Hermon. They built their towns and planted their crops by the icy waters that flowed to the Sea of Galilee and the Dead Sea via the Jordan River.

Over 2,700 m. (9,000 ft.) high, Mount Hermon juts against the horizon to the northeast. Snow covers its highest peaks until midsummer. The mountain can be seen from a remarkable distance. One visitor told of distinguishing the white snowcap of Mount

Wadi Far'a. *Wadi* is the Arabic word for a dry ravine that fills with water in the rainy season. There are numerous wadis throughout Israel. The Wadi Far'a, shown here, lies near the Judean city of Anathoth, the home of the prophet Jeremiah.

Hermon above the Golan Heights from the western side of the Jordan Valley—a distance of 97 km. (60 mi.)!

The imposing heights, abundant water, and luxurious vegetation struck awe in the hearts of those who settled in the shadows of the Hermon range. Even before the Israelites came, Canaanites linked the region with their fertility god, Baal. Part of the range is called Baal-hermon (Judg. 3:3; 1 Chron. 5:23), and there is a city of Baal-gad (Josh. 13:5).

Idolatrous Israelites viewed Mount Hermon as a fertility symbol, as the pagan Canaanites did. But the Israelites credited fertility and might to the Creator, not to His creation. To them, the power and magnificence of God dwarfed even the mighty peaks of the north—Lebanon, Tabor, and Hermon: "The voice of the LORD breaketh the cedars; yea, the LORD breaketh the cedars of Lebanon. He maketh them also to skip like a calf; Lebanon and Sirion [Hermon] like a young unicorn (Psa. 29:5-6). In their eyes the mountains themselves worshiped Yahweh: "Tabor and Hermon shall rejoice in thy name" (Psa. 89:12).

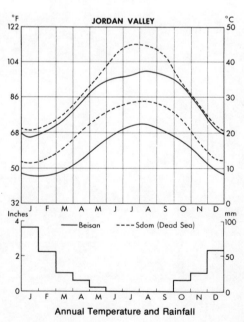

Annual Temperature and Rainfall

The many names of Mount Hermon show its importance. Before the Israelites conquered them, the Amorites called it Shenir (Deut. 3:9) or Mount Senir (Deut. 3:9; Ezek. 27:5). To the people of Sidon it was Mount Sirion (Deut. 3:9), and the Hebrew of Deuteronomy 4:48 refers to it as Mount Sion, though the Syriac version has Sirian.

When war threatened Israel's northern border, the Hermon range absorbed the first shock of invading forces. With the Lebanon mountains to the west, it provided a natural barrier

Snow in Jerusalem. A little snow may fall once or twice during Jerusalem's rainy season, but it usually melts quickly. A very heavy snowfall occurs about once in 15 years. The Israelites welcome the wet weather, despite the discomfort it brings, because rain and snow will improve the next season's harvest.

to the Aramaean kingdom of the north. But in times of peace the great Mount Hermon still helped the people of Canaan. She quietly gave birth to springs around her base, as melting snows seeped through the porous rocks that make up her foundation.

2. Sources of the Jordan. The Jordan River begins in the Hula Valley of Northern Palestine. Actually, four rivers—the Senir, Dan, Ayyon, and Hermon—flowed into Hula Lake and their waters emerged at the southern tip of the lake as the Jordan River.

Springs in the northern recesses of Lebanon created the Senir River. These springs are situated 52 km. (32 mi.) northeast of Metulla, Israel's northernmost settlement, and are fed by runoff water from the western slope of Mount Hermon.

A larger river, the Dan, comes from the ancient springs of Dan. Here the water flows into a crystal pool of ice-cold water and drops quickly into rapids. Smaller springs in the area ooze out of the ground and trickle from the rocks to water the dense foliage of mosses, bushes, and trees.

The tribe of Dan scouted this land and decided it was an ideal spot to settle. So they wiped out the peaceful inhabitants of Laish, rebuilt the town, and renamed it Dan. Instead of going to worship at Shiloh, about 128 km. (80 mi.) away, they set up their own shrine with stolen idols (Judg. 18).

The Ayyon River (which in biblical times drained the Ayyon Valley in Lebanon) contains Palestine's most impressive waterfall, the Tannur. At Abel-beth-maacah, a mile south of the waterfall,

21

King David's men besieged that "worthless fellow" Sheba who drew away Israel's allegiance with his cry: "We have no part in David" (2 Sam. 20:1).

The fourth river feeding into the Jordan River, the Hermon, spills from beneath a high rock wall at what was once the village of Banias. The Banias springs were originally named *Paneas* after Pan, Greek god of forests and meadows. *Banias* reflects the Roman term for *bath*.

Herod the Great built a temple at Banias and dedicated the site to Caesar Augustus. Later the tetrarch Philip made his home there and renamed it Caesarea Philippi, after himself.

At Caesarea Philippi, a profusion of rocks was scattered along the river bank. Idols were nestled in the niches of a high rock wall dedicated to Pan. In the Master's powerful way He welded the setting to His response: "Blessed art thou, Simon Bar-jona....thou art Peter, and upon this rock I will build my church; and the gates of hell shall not prevail against it" (Matt. 16:17-18).

What a contrast! Peter voiced his faith in Christ amid rampant paganism and Rome's worldly might. Yet on the rock of Peter's confession all other rocks—the power of Rome included—would crumble.

Mount Hermon. Over 2700 m. (9,000 ft.) high, Mount Hermon rises above the floor of the Upper Jordan Valley, marking the northern boundary between the Israelites and the Amorites. Snowcapped for most of the year, the mountain is visible from a remarkable distance.

The Jordan River. The Hebrew name of the Jordan River literally means "the descender." Beginning 70 m. (230 ft.) above sea level, it drops to 213 m. (700 ft.) below sea level 16 km. (10 mi.) south of the Sea of Galilee. By the time it reaches the northern end of the Dead Sea, the river has plunged to 393 m. (1,290 ft.) below sea level. The distance of about 120 km. (75 mi.) from its source to the Dead Sea is more than doubled by the river's meandering. No other river figures more prominently in the Bible.

Since they were traveling in the region of Caesarea Philippi, Jesus might have led Peter and James to one of Mount Hermon's ridges to witness His transfiguration. (Some believe the "high mountain" of Matthew 17:1 was Mount Tabor, but the preceding passage places the group near Mount Hermon.)

3. Hula Lake. Hula Lake nestles close to the Lebanon and Hermon ranges in the Upper Jordan Valley. In Bible times, river waters drained into the shallow water of the Hula swamps, and then into the lake. The swamps north of the lake were filled with semitropical plants. Alligators, hippopotamuses, and water buffalo made their homes there. Since drainage was poor, settlers often contracted malaria, and at certain seasons the area flooded. With so many hazards, the land was not fully used.

A layer of basalt blocked the southern end of Hula Lake. Volcanic activity in the Golan Heights had dumped lava on the mountains north of Galilee. These areas were equally hostile to settlers.

In Old Testament times, river water cut a canal 16 km. (10 mi.) through the basalt. The canal drops 750 feet in that stretch and deepens as it goes. Consequently, travelers could cross the Jordan at only one point of the canal, just below the lake. Travelers who were willing to wait until the water was low could ford the river there. Caravans loaded with wares from Egypt and Israel regularly crossed the Jordan at that ford on their way north to Damascus or Mesopotamia.

In our time, the Bridge of the Daughters of Jacob spans the ancient ford. Modern Israeli tanks and trucks loaded with ammunition rumble over it to reach the Golan Heights.

Twentieth-century Israelis have made other changes in the region as well. From 1951 to 1958 they drained Hula Lake and reclaimed over 78,000 sq. km. (20,000 acres) of highly fertile land from the lake bed and swamps. They also straightened and deepened the canal to the Sea of Galilee.

B. The Jordan Valley Proper. The Jordan River Valley stretches out in the middle of Palestine for 105 km. (65 mi.). Elevation drops gradually as the Jordan leaves the Sea of Galilee at an altitude of 195 m. (650 ft.) below sea level and enters the Dead Sea at 387 m. (1,290 ft.) below sea level. Since the river depth varies and the water is full of sandbars, sailors do not try to navigate between the two seas.

About 8 km. (5 mi.) south of the Sea of Galilee, the Jordan doubles in size as the Yarmuk River adds roughly 459,000 cu. m. (16.2 million cu. ft.) of water to its flow every minute. Other rivers such as the Jabbok swell the Jordan by an additional 94,500 cu. m. (3.3 million cu. ft.) per minute.

The watercourse of the Jordan is everchanging. The entire Jordan Valley was once under water. This left debris of loose soil and gravel, especially to the south in a land now called the *qattara* or "badlands." Little rivers feed soil as well as water into the Jordan, and its own currents eat away the riverbed. Earthquakes and tremors have dumped dirt into the river also, sometimes blocking the Jordan's flow and forcing it to seek a new course.

Desolate mountain ranges flank the river. To the west, Samaria and Bethel reach 450 m. (1,500 ft.) in Lower Galilee. East of the Jordan, the humps of the gilead rise to 600 m. (2,000 ft.).

At one point the valley is only 3 km. (2 mi.) wide. It spreads out to 11 km. (7 mi.) near Beth-shean and the Jezreel Valley, and by Jericho it widens to a span of 22.5 km. (14 mi.). A narrow pass in the hill country of Samaria separates the Jordan Valley into the Beth-shean and Lower Jordan valleys.

1. A Natural Boundary. The Jordan River served Canaan as a natural boundary, holding back eastern invaders.

From the Book of Genesis onward, the Scriptures speak of the Jordan River as a boundary or border. Several Scripture texts refer to crossing the Jordan; Genesis 32:10; Deuteronomy 3:20, 25; 27:4; Joshua 1:1; Numbers 34:10-12.

As the tribes of Israel moved north from the Sinai, they approached the Jordan Valley from the east. At the time, plundering tribes from the desert controlled that land, and the Jordan was a frontier. Three tribes wanted to stay and graze their cattle there, but Moses urged them to go across the Jordan to help in the conquest of Canaan. They did so, with the provision that after the conquest they could return to the eastern shore to settle. The tribes of Reuben and Gad and half the tribe of Manasseh eventually re-

Jabbok River. The Jabbok flows westward into the Jordan River about 32 km. (20 mi.) north of the Dead Sea. Over 96 km. (60 mi.) long, it is known as the Wadi Zerqa today. The river marked a boundary line between Ammon and the tribes of Reuben and Gad (Deut. 3:16). It was also the river that Jacob forded when he wrestled with the angel (Gen. 32).

The Five Distinct Regions of Palestine

While some scholars see merit in dividing Palestine into many more areas, five distinct regions can be identified easily.

The Coastal Plain. Between the sea and a hilly plateau to the west lies an alluvial plain. About 140 miles in length, it reaches from the southern edge of Lebanon to Gaza, gradually widening as it moves southward. Near its beginning in the north it is interrupted by Mount Carmel. From this mountain extending south and east runs the valley of Jezreel and the plain of Esdraelon, providing a gateway to Canaan or Israel and Judah.

The Central Hill Country. This region might be called the spine or backbone of the country. Through its length runs an imaginary line from Dan to Beersheba, a distance of some 160 miles. Extending the line to Kadesh-Barnea, the southern limit of Israel's effective control of the land, adds another twenty to thirty miles and takes the traveler out of the central hill country into the desert. The entire central area is made up of interlocking hills and plateaus, beginning with an elevation of more than 3,000 feet in the north, broken by the valley of Jezreel, but rising again into small hills in southern Galilee and Samaria. In lower Samaria or Ephraim, the hill country, elevations again climb to above 1,000 feet. In the east the Judean hills drop off sharply into the Rift Valley west of the Dead Sea.

The Rift Valley. Like a great gash in the earth's crust, the Rift Valley slices through Palestine from north to south. The Rift is marked by Lake Huleh, the upper Jordan, the Sea of Galilee, and lower Jordan meandering in winding loops and twists to meet its fate in the waters of the Dead Sea. The Jordan is called the "Descender;" its tortuous journey takes it from the mountain slopes of lofty Mt. Hermon to the lowest spot on the earth's face.

The Transjordan Plateau. East of the Jordan, rising sharply above the Rift Valley is a high tableland. Receiving some rainfall, it is broken by three rivers or streams: the Yarmuk; the Jabbock, which flows into the Jordan above its mouth; and the Arnon which drains itself directly into the Dead Sea. The area south and east of Galilee along the Yarmuk was ancient Bashan, in New Testament times called Decapolis. South, across the Yarmuk, lay Gilead. Even further south was Ammon and Moab. East of the Dead Sea, with the Arnon flowing through, was Edom with its impregnable strongholds.

The Desert. Toward the east, the rainfall enjoyed by Transjordan rapidly plays out. It turns into a desert, volcanic in character with lava flows outcropping in low hills. Everywhere on the east, the land is bordered by this desert. To the south, it again finds its limits in deserts. These are different, however; they are dunes of sand. Since they offer no topographical barriers, they have furnished a gateway for many invaders and predators. The desert itself is a predator; it sends its sand into southern and southeastern Judea.

THE FIVE
DISTINCT REGIONS
OF PALESTINE

CENTRAL

HILL

COASTAL

PLAINS

JORDAN RIFT VALLEY

TRANSJORDAN PLATEAU

COUNTRY

DESERT

Mount Tabor. Rising from the Plain of Jezreel to almost 600 m. (1,000 ft.), Mount Tabor is located on the tribal boundary between Zebulun and Issachar. There is a magnificent view from the summit, where an idolatrous shrine was set up during Hosea's day (*ca.* 730 B.C.).

ceived their inheritance east of the river, as they had requested. Still, the prospect of being separated from the other tribes troubled them: "In time to come your children might speak unto our children, saying, What have ye to do with the LORD God of Israel? For the LORD hath made Jordan a border between us and you, ye children of Reuben and children of Gad; ye have no part in the LORD: so shall your children make our children cease from fearing the LORD" (Josh. 22:24-25).

Many gospel songs have been written about going over the Jordan, and with good reason. It was not an easy river to cross. The Israelites could ford the Jordan at traditional spots, and even those places were useless when the Jordan flooded its banks.

The Israelites knew the value of the fords and wrested them from their enemies as soon as possible. Ehud's forces "took the fords of Jordan toward Moab, and suffered not a man to pass over" (Judg. 3:28). Gideon recruited men for his army with the cry, "Come down against the Midianites and take before them the waters" (Judg. 7:24).

For the most part, the Jordan Valley was sparsely settled, partly because of the heat and dryness. More people settled in the Beth-shean Valley to the north, where it was at least possible to irrigate crops.

2. The Beth-shean Valley. Tributaries on both sides of the Jordan flood their banks in winter and spring. Though the climate in the Beth-shean Valley resembles a desert, the plentiful amount of water and high temperatures produce dense subtropical brush.

The Israelis eventually dug canals to control the flooding and used the Jordan's waters to irrigate crops in the valley.

A modern city of 15,000 people, Beth-shean lies at the foot of Mount Gilboa 24 km. (15.5 mi.) south of the Sea of Galilee where the Valley of Jezreel meets the Jordan Valley.

C. The Lower Jordan. The Lower Jordan Valley contains three distinct levels. They appear on both sides of the river, and are known as the *zor*, the *qattara*, and the *ghor*.

Closest to the river is the *zor*, a narrow strip of land one or two miles wide, which the Bible calls the "thickets of the Jordan" or the wilderness. Thanks to seasonal floods, the zor was a veritable jungle of dense brush, shrubs, and tamarisk trees. Wild beasts hid in its shelter. Jeremiah speaks of "a lion from the swelling of Jordan" (Jer. 49:19). The sons of the prophets were cutting down trees in the Jordan thickets when Elisha made an iron axe head float on the river (2 Kings 6:1-7).

John the Baptist prepared the way for the Messiah in the zor near Jericho: "John did baptize in the wilderness, and preach the

Sea of Galilee. Located in the northern part of the Jordan Valley, the Sea of Galilee is really a lake 24 km. (15 mi.) long and 10 km. (6 mi.) wide. This body of water is called the "Sea of Chinnereth" in Numbers 34:11 and the "lake of Gennesaret" in Luke 5:1. Christ's ministry often took Him to the towns on its shores. This photograph shows the southern portion of the lake, where the Jordan River leaves it; the mountains of Syria are in the background.

baptism of repentance for the remission of sins" (Mark 1:4). He also baptized Jesus in the Jordan (1:9).

Away from the river, beyond the zor, are the *qattara* badlands. This territory is covered by ancient deposits of sediment from the lake that once filled the Jordan Valley. Seasonal streams carve deep crevices in the *qattara*. No one grew crops there because the soil was salty. Modern Israeli scientists are reclaiming the soil by washing it with river water.

The *ghor* is a steep but fertile terrace between the *qattara* and the mountains. Farmers irrigate and cultivate these fields.

GALILEE

Jesus proclaimed the Good News in the lowlands of Galilee. The prophet Isaiah had predicted that He would minister in "The land of Zebulun, and the land of Naphtali, by the way of the sea, beyond Jordan, Galilee of the Gentiles" (Matt. 4:15).

Volcanoes and earthquakes shaped the landscape of Galilee. The area holds isolated mountains, high plateaus, valleys and gorges, rocky ridges and steep cliffs. Galilee divides naturally into two parts, with obvious differences in altitude, climate, and vegetation.

A. Upper Galilee. Upper Galilee lies south and west of the Hula Valley. It extends eastward from the Mediterranean Sea to the town of Safed, and south to the Beth-haccerem Valley. In this fertile valley live olive trees that are hundreds of years old.

At one time Upper Galilee was probably a single block of mountain, but massive natural forces split it into many pieces. Some parts were thrust up, others sank down, and all were eroded by water.

The tribe of Naphtali settled the mountainous area to the east. From the Naphtali Range (about 600 m. or 2,000 ft. above sea level), the traveler gets a splendid view of the Hula Valley. The scattered peaks of Mount Meiron, Mount Shammai (or Mount Hillel), and the Mount Ha-ari, rising between 1,000 and 1,200 m. (3,400 to 3,900 ft.), tower above the relatively high mountain ranges of Upper Galilee.

Few people settled in Upper Galilee. The rugged mountains and sharp cliffs mostly offered protection for fugitives and refugees. King Solomon gave twenty cities in the northwestern territory to King Hiram of Tyre. But the biblical timber baron didn't appreciate the gift: "And Hiram came out from Tyre to see the cities which Solomon had given him; and they pleased him not. And he said, What cities are these which thou hast given me, my brother? And he called them the land of Cabul unto this day" (1 Kings 9:12-13). Roughly translated, *Cabul* meant "obscurity." Hiram's discourteous remark immediately strained relations with his new subjects in the cities of Galilee.

On Upper Galilee's eastern border stands the modern city of Safed, 540 mi. (1,800 ft.) above sea level. Safed is visible from the northern shore of the Sea of Galilee. The twinkling night lights of such a town might have prompted Jesus' remark: "A city that is set on a hill cannot be hid" (Matt. 5:14).

B. Lower Galilee. Lower Galilee is literally lower than Upper Galilee, being a plateau about 350 feet above sea level. In Lower Galilee we find Jesus' hometown (Matt. 2:23). Nazareth perches atop a steeply tilted hunk of earth. It seems impossible to enter Nazareth from the south, but a tenacious road curves and twists up the narrow ridge into the city. The attempt made on Jesus' life at Nazareth no doubt occurred on the cliffs to the south: "And they

Judean Wilderness. The Judean Wilderness mentioned in Judges 11:6 is probably identical with the wilderness of Judah, a desert to the west of the Dead Sea and to the east of the Judean hill country. Sharp outcroppings of bare rocks pierce the desolate and barren stretches of rolling sands. Hot, dusty winds shift the dunes about. Rain seldom falls here.

rose up and put him out of the city, and led him to the brow of the hill on which their city was built, that they might throw him down headlong. But passing through the midst of them he went away" (Luke 4:29-30, RSV).

Looking away from Nazareth, one sees Mount Tabor, a cone-shaped volcanic mountain almost 600 m. (2,000 ft.) high. In the days of the judges, Deborah sent Barak and his troops to Mount Tabor to attack the Canaanites (Jer. 4:6). Jeremiah evoked the name to pronounce doom on Egypt: "Surely as Tabor is among the mountains, and as Carmel by the sea, so shall he come" (Jer. 46:18).

Mount Tabor's beautiful foliage contrasts with the rather barren grassy hills at its base. Some say that Mount Tabor was the site of Jesus' transfiguration. It is difficult to climb.

Another volcanic crater, the Horns of Hittin, can be seen from many parts of Galilee. In A.D. 1187 a decisive battle took place there between the Crusaders and the Arab leader Saladin.

Earthquakes produced two other mountains in Galilee that are really escarpments: long cliff-like ridges. Mount Arbel rises only to 180 m. (600 ft.), yet from it one can see the arena of Jesus' ministry: the valley of Gennosar, the Mount of the Beatitudes, Capernaum, and the blue waters of the Sea of Galilee, and the Golan Heights beyond. Wadi Arbel served as a junction between the road of Galilee (from Hazor and Damascus) and the Horns of Hittim.

The second escarpment overlooks the Jordan Valley, Golan Heights, and the Sea of Galilee. Though Ramat Kokav is the highest mountain in Lower Galilee, the Scriptures do not mention it. But the Crusaders built a fortress on its summit. They named the stronghold *Belvoir* (good lookout point), because of the excellent view which includes even the snow-capped peaks of Mount Hermon.

C. The Sea of Galilee. Many people think of this as a large body of water. Actually, the Sea of Galilee is a lake below sea level, and not a very large one. Roughly pear-shaped, the water is only 10 km. (6 mi.) wide and 24 km. (15 mi.) from north to south. It is 39 to 47 m. (120 to 155 ft.) deep, and its surface is 206 m. (650 ft.) below sea level. Its circumference is about 51 km. (32 mi.). It is listed as the Lake (or Sea) of Chinnereth on Old Testament maps. Later it was called Lake Gennesaret (Luke 5:1), the Sea of Tiberias (John 6:1), or most frequently, the Sea of Galilee.

The territories of Naphtali, Zebulun, and Issachar bordered Lake Chinnereth in Old Testament times. They constituted the region of Galilee, a subdivision of the Northern Kingdom. Under Rome's rule, the provinces of Galilee, Judah, and Samaria were part of Herod's kingdom. Herod the Great supposedly rid Galilee of robbers and repopulated the north with Jews. Once known as "Galilee of the nations" (Isa. 9:1; RSV "Gentiles"), it became a vigorously Jewish region. Still, the people of Judea despised the Jews of Galilee. However, Jesus conducted most of his ministry in the vicinity of the Sea of Galilee.

Steep hills skirt most of the shoreline. Streams by Bethsaida, Gennesaret, and Sennabris created fertile valleys that the Israelites cultivated. They often built villages on hills and mountaintops. The Arbel cliffs above Magdala offer a panoramic view of the northern region of the lake. The map helps us visualize some familiar New Testament events.

"And Jesus, walking by the Sea of Galilee, saw two brethren, Simon called Peter, and Andrew his brother, casting a net into the sea: for they were fishers" (Matt. 4:18).

About 3.5 km. (2 mi.) west of Capernaum stands the Hill of the Beatitudes, where Jesus may have delivered the Sermon on the Mount (Matt. 5). On one of these hills He fed the 5,000 with a few loaves and fishes.

When Nazareth rejected Jesus (Luke 4:29-31), He made Capernaum the center of his ministry. Jesus taught in their synagogue, performed many miracles, and then set out on a preaching mission. After the Resurrection, Jesus returned to the shores of Galilee.

SAMARIA

North of the Dead Sea and west of the Jordan is the hill country of Samaria. A harsh, mountainous land full of fissures and valleys, its boundaries run from the Jordan Valley on the east to the Plain of Sharon on the west. The valleys of Jezreel and Esdraelon border it on the north. The southern boundaries tended to shift, since there is no sharp division between the hill country of Samaria and that of Judah.

If you were to stand on Mount Nebo and look westward across the Jordan, Samaria might appear to be an impenetrable mountain mass. From the floor of the Jordan Valley, 240 m. (800 ft.) below sea level, the Samarian hills climb steeply to 600 m. (2,000 ft.) above sea level within 11 km. (7 mi.). The coastal side drops more gradually, taking 40 km. (25 mi.) to descend to sea level. Understandably the west offers easier ways into the hill country of Samaria than the passes of the east.

Mountain passes made Samaria's hills accessible and connected the country with other towns and peoples. Several important routes passed through Samaria. One road passes Beth-shean north of Mount Gilboa to Megiddo, connecting Samaria to the Via Maris, Canaan's major north-south highway. Just west of Mount Gilboa one branch heads south, passing through the Valley of Dothan. Northeast of Shechem is the pass of Wadi Far'a by which a traveler can reach the Jordan Valley. The Wadi Far'a descends gradually 300 m. in 16 km. (or 1,000 ft. in 10 miles), compared to the steep cliffs (750 m. or 2,500 ft.) through which it passes.

The Via Maris ran parallel to the main watershed of the Samarian hill country in the Plain of Sharon. From early times, settlers of

Samaria. The ancient capital of the northern kingdom of Israel, Samaria was ideally situated amid fertile hills at the junction of important roads. A natural acropolis made this a strategic military site. This view shows the gentle contours of the surrounding countryside, so different from the harsh landscapes of Judea.

the hill country maintained connections with the coastal highway for trade and cultural purposes.

Many place names of Samaria are familiar to Bible readers. At Shechem both Abraham and Jacob built altars (Gen. 12:6-8; 33:18). There the Israelites buried Joseph's bones (Josh. 24:32) and renewed the covenant God had made with Moses.

Remember when the lad Joseph went to look for his brothers? He found them in the Valley of Dothan (Gen. 37:17). Several judges were active in the region: Deborah, Gideon, Tola, and Abdon. The first prophet, Samuel, grew up at the Tabernacle of Shiloh. Later he made his birthplace, Ramah, his headquarters and traveled a circuit that included the towns of Bethel, Gilgal, and Mizpah (1 Sam. 1:1-2:11; 7:15-17).

The northern kingdom of Israel made Samaria its capital, and many battles were fought in its open valleys. Such characters as Ahab, Elijah, Jehu, and Elisha appeared in this hilly country to play important parts in the history of Israel.

At the northern tip of Samaria is Mount Gilboa, a significant place in Israel's military history. Here the Lord once instructed Gideon to reduce his forces from 32,000 to 300 men so it would be obvious that God was responsible for their victory against the Midianites and Amalekites. The "people of the East" had crossed the Jordan and camped in the valley of Jezreel, by the hill of Moreh. Gideon's forces camped near the spring of Harod, at the foot of Mount Gilboa. Gideon obeyed the Lord, and his tiny army routed the enemy (Judg. 7:1-25).

In a later battle, Saul did not fare as well. "Now the Philistines fought against Israel: and the men of Israel fled from before the Philistines, and fell down slain in Mount Gilboa" (1 Sam. 31:1). Saul's sons were killed in the battle, and Saul committed suicide. The Philistines hung the bodies of Saul and the royal sons on the wall of Beth-shean in the Harod Valley (31:10). On hearing of their deaths, David lamented: "Ye mountains of Gilboa, let there be no dew, neither let there be rain, upon you...for there the shield of the mighty is vilely cast away, the shield of Saul, as though he had not been anointed with oil" (2 Sam. 1:21).

Jesus also visited Samaria. In fact, it was at Jacob's well near Shechem that He met the "woman of Samaria" (John 4:5-7).

Samaria was one of three specific places named in the Great

Commission Jesus gave just before His ascension: "Ye shall be witnesses unto me both in Jerusalem, and in all Judea, and in Samaria, and unto the uttermost part of the earth" (Acts 1:8). When the early church was scattered by the persecution in Jerusalem, Philip took the gospel to Samaria, where it was well received (Acts 8:1-6, 14).

JUDAH

No one can say for certain where the land of Samaria ended and Judah began. Some say the road from Ajalon to Jericho, passing between Bethel and Gibeon, marks the boundary. Others think Samaria ended with the road from Beth-shemesh to Jerusalem. Between the two were the Bethel hills, the shifting border of the northern kingdom of Israel.

Judah encompasses a spine of mountains and the barren desert sands of the wilderness. The hill country of Judah runs parallel to the plateau of Moab which lies on the other side of the Dead Sea. It goes roughly in a northeast-southwest direction from Bethel to Hebron, with the mountains tapering off in the south, at Beersheba. The mountains are even higher than those of Samaria, rising to 990 m. (3,300 ft.).

A. Bethel Hills. The Bible says little of the Bethel hills, though the tribes of Benjamin and Ephraim settled in this region. Manasseh to the north and Judah to the south are mentioned more frequently in the Scriptures. Yet the Bethel hills contained fertile valleys, such as the plateau between Gibeon and Michmash. Since rainfall was heavy, the region was soon cultivated.

B. Jerusalem Hills. South of the Bethel hills, in line with the northern tip of the Dead Sea, are the Jerusalem hills and the city of Jerusalem. The city lies 600 m. (about 2,000 ft.) above sea level, and the hills that surround it are lower than those of Bethel or Hebron. "As the mountains are round about Jerusalem," said the Psalmist, "so the LORD is round about his people" (Psa. 125:2a). Even from 13 km. (8 mi.) away, Jerusalem can be seen from the encircling mountains.

Ravines cut Jerusalem off from all directions but the north, for several valleys converge at this location.

Jerusalem. The recently discovered Ebla Tablets contain the earliest known reference to Jerusalem, indicating that the city existed in the early second millennium B.C. Some scholars think this is the city called "Salem" in Genesis 14. This aerial photograph shows the large open space surrounding the dome-topped Mosque of Omar built on what is thought to be the site of the Holy of Holies in Solomon's Temple.

When Jesus came to Jerusalem, the palaces of Herod and the high priest Caiaphas were within the walled city. From their windows they could look down upon the Valley of Hinnom, to the west. King Ahaz had "burned his sons as an offering in the valley of the son of Hinnom, and practiced soothsaying and augury and sorcery, and dealt with mediums and with wizards. He did much evil in the sight of the LORD, provoking him to anger" (2 Chron. 33:6, RSV). Jesus used the name of the region (*Ge-hinnom*, in Greek *Gehenna*) for hell, the ultimate place of God's judgment. Judas, it seems, committed suicide in this valley.

By the Pool of Siloam the Hinnom and Kidron Valleys come together. The Kidron River runs between the Mount of Olives and the Hill of Jerusalem, also known as Mount Moriah. The events of history mingle in Jerusalem, for it was on Mount Moriah that Abraham prepared to sacrifice Isaac (Gen. 22:2), and where the Lord appeared to David (2 Chron. 3:1). From the confluence of the Hinnom and Kidron Rivers, rainwater flows through the Judean wilderness to the Dead Sea.

C. Hebron Hills. If we continue our journey south, we approach the Hebron range. At over 900 m. (3000 ft.), it is the highest range in Judah. On Hebron's slopes Abraham and Isaac tended their flocks. Near Hebron, Abraham purchased the Cave of Machpelah to bury Sarah, and the patriarchs were also interred there. After Saul's death, David ruled Judah from Hebron for about seven years before he captured Jerusalem.

D. The Coastal Plains. Alongside the mountain ranges of Judah and Samaria lies the coast of the beautiful Mediterranean Sea. It is a remarkably smooth coastline. Sea currents straightened much of the shoreline by depositing sand picked up from the Nile delta. Northward, the sand deposits decrease until, by the Ladder of Tyre, the coast is rocky.

Between sand deposits and rocks, it seemed impossible to develop a harbor for international shipping until late in Israel's history. The Phoenicians used the natural harbors at Sidon and Tyre, but on Palestine's stretch of the Mediterranean, only small vessels could dock at Joppa. Solomon's main harbor was Ezion-geber, on the Red Sea's Gulf of Eilat. Other kings of Judah unsuccessfully contested the Edomites for control of that region.

During the rule of Herod the Great, the Romans developed two more ports, Ptolemaïs (Acre) and Caesarea. The Apostle Paul docked at Caesarea at the close of his second missionary journey, then visited both Ptolemais and Caesarea after his third journey. Later, Festus sent Paul from Caesarea to Rome as a prisoner (Acts 27:2).

Philistine Coast. This section of Palestine's Mediterranean coast is located near the ruins of the Philistine city Ashkelon. There are few natural seaports along this coast, which explains why ancient Israel never became a seafaring nation.

Wadi Mughara, Mount Carmel. The caves at this site contain evidence of human occupation during the Paleolithic period (before 800 B.C.). Mount Carmel is the name given to the main ridge of the Carmel range about 28 km. (12 mi.) inland from the Mediterranean Sea. Mount Carmel marked the border of Asher (Josh. 19:26).

The Palestinian coast has extensive deposits of *kurkar*, a type of sandstone. Kurkar disintegrates slowly and hardens when it meets water, so it tends to prevent erosion of the shoreline. Little islands of kurkar and a sandstone ridge follow the coastline by Samaria. Until modern times, the Sharon Plain was swampy because that ridge held back water draining from the Samarian hills. Thus the water flooded the plain, where rivers slowly carried it to the sea.

E. The Philistine Coast. The Philistines controlled the coast from the Yarkon River (near Joppa) to Gaza. Dune belts skirt the shore, especially to the south. The dunes are approximately 6 km. (4 mi.) wide by Gaza, and south of the Philistine Coast the sand extends even farther inland. A fertile plain about 16 km. (10 mi.) wide lies east of the dunes. Sediment and sand create a rich soil, and many types of crops are grown there.

In this region the Philistines lived and worshiped.

Five major cities controlled Philistia and its trade routes. To go from Phoenicia to Egypt, or through Israel's Shephelah into the Judean hills, traders had to pass through Philistia. Gaza, Ashdod, and Ashkelon were near the coast and served as small harbors. Gath and Ekron were further inland, on a road running parallel to the Via Maris. Goliath, the Philistine giant, came from Gath.

F. The Shephelah. The Shephelah, a strip of land 13 by 64 km. (8 by 40 mi.) between Philistia's coastal plain and the Judean hills, was a much-disputed territory. Its low-lying hills are mostly of chalk, which easily erodes to form passes and caves. The most important pass into the hills is the Valley of Ajalon, where Joshua said, "Sun, stand thou still upon Gibeon; and thou, Moon, in the valley of Ajalon" (Josh. 10:12).

Judah could have been quite isolated, except for the Philistines on the west. International roads crossed through Samaria, but the coastal plains insulated Judah's hills from the Via Maris ("Road to the Sea") thoroughfare. Judah could easily check traffic on the road from Shechem to Jerusalem, and in times of war with Israel she simply closed the northern border. The Judean Desert to the east and the Negev Desert on the south helped isolate the southern kingdom.

But that vulnerable western front remained. The kings of Judah poured much effort and expense into strengthening the fortified cities of the Shephelah. It was Solomon's idea to flank Jerusalem with defense cities, such as Gezer and Beth-horon (1 Kings 9:15-17). Rehoboam, Abijah, Asa, and Jehoshaphat also reinforced Judah's western frontier (2 Chron. 11:5-12, 23; 13:7; 14:6 f.; 17:1 ff.).

A modern traveler can still take one of the two roads that led from the domain of the five Philistine kings into the heart of Saul's kingdom in the Shephelah. One road passes through Lachish, one of Judah's military defense centers, then leads northward into the Valley of Elah. The other originates farther north at Ashdod, passes by Gath, and reaches the valley of Elah after a journey of 32 km. (20 mi.). Merging in the valley, the roads con-

TRANSJORDAN

• Damascus

▲ Mt. Hermon

Sea of Galilee

Yarmuk River

• Jabesh-Gilead

Jordan River

Jabbok River

• Ramoth-Gilead

• Heshbon

© Thomas Nelson, Inc.

tinue northward via Beth-horon and Gibeon to Michmash, an ancient outpost of the Philistines (1 Sam. 13:5). Saul's son Jonathan boldly routed the Philistine forces at the pass of Michmash, forcing them to retreat to the Valley of Ajalon (1 Sam. 14:1-31).

One of the most famous biblical dramas was staged in the Valley of Elah: "Now the Philistines gathered together their armies to battle, and were gathered together at Shochoh, which belongeth to Judah, and pitched between Shochoh and Azekah, in Ephesdammim. And Saul and the men of Israel were gathered together, and pitched by the valley of Elah, and set the battle in array against the Philistines. And the Philistines stood on a mountain on the one side, and Israel stood on a mountain on the other side: and there was a valley between them. And there went out a champion out of the camp of the Philistines, named Goliath" (1 Sam. 17:1-4).

The newly anointed king, David, heard the challenge as he brought supplies to his brothers. Over the protests of his brothers and despite King Saul's reservations, David met Goliath. His only assurance was: "The LORD that delivered me out of the paw of the lion, and out of the paw of the bear, he will deliver me out of the hand of this Philistine" (17:37).

The first stone he slung felled the giant, and the Israelites chased the astonished Philistines all the way back to the coastal plains.

G. The Sharon and Carmel Coast. The Philistine territory ended at the Yarkon River, where the Plain of Sharon begins. Largest of the coastal plains, the Sharon reaches to the Crocodile River in the north.

Though it seemed to be too swampy and shrub-filled to be much good for human settlement, the Sharon Valley was quite fertile, according to the Old Testament. The region was best suited for pasturage (Isa. 65:10), and in it the "Rose of Sharon" grew wild (Song of Sol. 2:1). Isaiah spoke of the "excellency of Carmel and Sharon" (Isa. 35:2). Perhaps the Israelites regarded the extensive swamps of the Sharon much as we today value America's wilderness regions.

A few cities dotted the Plain: Shocho (1 Kings 4:10), Gilgal (Josh. 10:7), Aphek, Gathrimmon, Lod, and Ono (1 Chron. 8:12). A small harbor at Dor provided international contacts for the Canaanites.

H. The Plain of Asher. According to the prophetess Deborah, the tribe of Asher "continued on the seashore, and abode in his breaches" (Judg. 5:17b). This small plain hugs the coast above the Plain of Sharon. For the most part, the Asher Valley is about five miles wide, though it widens south of the port of Accho (modern Acre). At the north end, the mountains of Galilee almost touch the sea, leaving a narrow passage to Phoenicia known as the Ladder of Tyre.

Because of its strategic location between Phoenicia and Egypt, the plain was important to commerce. In times of peace, the tribe of Asher enjoyed cultural prosperity, but during wars it suffered devastation.

THE DEAD SEA

The lowest body of water in the world is the Dead Sea, an oblong lake three-fourths as long as the Jordan Valley north of it. Eighty km. (50 mi.) in length, it does not measure more than 18 km. (11 mi.) at the widest; across from the Lisan Peninsula it narrows to 3 km. (2 mi.) or less.

THE DEAD SEA

The water surface of the Dead Sea is about 390 m. (1,300 ft.) below sea level. Its depth has been estimated at another 1,300 feet.

Tourists enjoy floating on the incredibly buoyant water of the Dead Sea. Because the sea has no outlet and evaporation is high, the concentration of minerals is as much as 30 percent. The water abounds with salt, bromide, magnesium chloride, potassium chloride, and sulfur. Modern Israelis mine the chemical salts of the rich waters for potash, bromine,

The Arabah. Derived from a Hebrew word meaning "steppe" or "desert," *Arabah* is the name given to the southern extension of the Jordan Valley. This depression extends more than 160 km. (100 mi.) from the Dead Sea to the Gulf of Aqaba.

and other industrial chemicals.

Long ago the Dead Sea was part of a huge inland lake that covered the Jordan Rift from the Hula Valley southward. A salt rock at Mount Sedom (at the southwest corner of the Dead Sea) and the *qattara* of the Jordan Valley are signs that eroding soil made the ancient lake more salty.

The level of the Dead Sea is dropping. In recent times both Israel and Jordan have diverted huge quantities of water from the Sea of Galilee and the Yarmuk River, so less water flows into it. At one time it was convenient to cross the Dead Sea by the Lisan Peninsula, where the water was about three feet deep. The water level has since dropped so much that only a narrow canal separates the western shore from the widening Lisan.

The third hottest temperature on world record (72 degrees C. or 129 degrees F.) was taken in this area on June 21, 1942. You would think no one would want to live where temperatures are so high, precipitation perhaps 5 cm. (2 in.) per year, and the scenery so bleak. Yet people have settled in this region from ancient times.

When Abraham and Lot went their separate ways, this region appeared fertile and desirable to Lot. Unfortunately for Lot, he moved into bad company. "But the men of Sodom were wicked and sinners before the LORD exceedingly" (Gen. 13:13). The tragic fate of Sodom and her sister city Gomorrah has been recalled by preachers from the Old Testament prophets down to the present day.

Archaeologists speculate that Sodom and Gomorrah were located in the southern portion of the Dead Sea. When the Lord reduced them to rubble because of their wickedness (Gen. 19), an earthquake probably dropped the land on which they stood and the waters of the Dead Sea inundated the debris.

In the midst of the Judean wasteland bordering the Dead Sea, the oases of En-gedi and Ein-Faschka provide food and springs of fresh water. Remains of an ancient temple show there was a settlement there as early as 4000 B.C. David and his men hid from Saul at En-gedi (1 Sam. 24:1). The Song of Solomon speaks of "a cluster of camphire in the vineyards of En-gedi" (Song of Sol. 1:14).

Near Ein-Faschka is the site of Qumran, where the Dead Sea Scrolls were found in 1947. During Jesus' time, this Essene community believed that they were the righteous remnant, sole heirs to God's covenant. They interpreted literally Isaiah's words: "The voice of him that crieth in the wilderness, Prepare ye the way of the LORD, make straight in the desert a highway for our God" (Isa. 40:3). Separating themselves for this purpose, they awaited the Lord's coming in the desert. The sweet waters at Ein-Faschka permitted vegetation to grow, supplying the community's physical needs.

The fortress of Masada overlooks the Dead Sea from the rocky

Qumran Cave. The harsh landscape of the Judean Wilderness is evident in this photograph of caves at Qumran just northwest of the Dead Sea and about 13 km. (8 mi.) south of Jericho. In these caves, archaeologists found the Dead Sea Scrolls, one of the greatest discoveries of biblical archaeology in this century.

Volcanic Pools. Just northeast of Capernaum, in the valleys that lace the Golan Heights, the volcanic pool of Berekhat Ha Meshushim reminds visitors of Palestine's geological origins. This natural swimming pool is surrounded by pentagonal lava formations. A cool mountain stream brings fresh water to the pool, which is a striking contrast to the barren hills around it.

Judean wilderness farther south. There the last Jewish forces of the Great Revolt took their own lives in A.D. 73, rather than submit to Rome's rule.

The Dead Sea region is aptly named. Even fish struggle against being carried into the sea, for its high mineral content brings immediate death. Yet the oases are a vivid reminder of how beautiful the region could be if the lake contained sweet water.

The prophet Ezekiel envisioned the restoration of the Dead Sea valley. In his vision, water poured forth from the temple altar and flowed into the Kidron through the Judean wilderness to the Dead Sea (Ezek. 47:8-12). Revelation 22:1-5 tells of a strikingly similar vision.

THE TRANSJORDAN

The term *Transjordan* means "on the other side of the Jordan," and in its widest sense this area includes all the land east of the Jordan River to the vast Syrian Desert. The area takes in the land east of the Upper Jordan Valley as well as that east and southeast of the Dead Sea—and everything in between. Today it includes the nations of Lebanon and Israel, and the Gaza Strip.

From a high vantage point in Palestine, the mountains of Transjordan seem to jump from the valley floor. Higher than Palestine's mountains (though no less bleak), their western rim gently runs down to the plateau of the desert.

Canyon-like riverbeds, running east and west, marked the divisions of tribal territory in Transjordan.

Bashan is the northern area between the Hermon and Yarmuk Rivers; Gilead lies between the Yarmuk and Jabbok. Next comes the land of the Ammonites (partly shared with the Moabites), whose southern border was the Arnon River. Moab extended from the Arnon to the Zered River. Finally, Edom stretched from the Zered to the Red Sea's Gulf of Eilat and the modern port of Aqaba.

A. Bashan. Bashan is the biblical name for an area that includes one of the modern world's political "hot spots," the Golan Heights, from which Syria shelled Ein Gev, precipitating Israel's Six-Day War in June 1967. This highly-coveted district follows the eastern side of the Upper Jordan Valley for about 64 km. (40 mi.), almost to Damascus.

In New Testament times, Herod the Great made Bashan's wheatlands the granary of the Near East. Even in the Old Testament era, the rich soil of this well-watered tract produced grain aplenty. Animal husbandry flourished, and the huge bulls and well-fed cows of Bashan were known far and wide. Exiled in the land of the Chaldeans, the prophet Ezekiel spoke of the "fatlings of Bashan" (Ezek. 39:18). Amos railed against the noblewomen of Samaria, calling them "cows of Bashan, who are in the mountain of Samaria, who oppress the poor, who crush the needy, who say to their husbands, 'Bring, that we may drink!' " (Amos 4:1, RSV). The Psalmist compared his enemies to the powerful beasts: "Many bulls have compassed me: strong bulls of Bashan have beset me round" (Psa. 22:12).

Mighty oaks grew in Bashan, Isaiah mentioned "all the cedars of Lebanon...all the oaks of Bashan" (Isa. 2:13). Though Lebanon's cedars were more highly prized than Bashan's oaks, the Israelites used the timber and even exported it. According to Ezekiel, the oaks of Bashan were used to make oars for Phoenician ships (Ezek. 27:6).

Ten cities in southern Bashan and northern Gilead organized to form the *Decapolis* mentioned in Matthew 4:25, as well as Mark 5:20 and 7:31. Each city was a strategic point in the political division of the region. Hippos, for instance, controlled the road to Damascus, for which Paul was heading to persecute early Christians when he was converted (Acts 9:3). Today that road overlooks the modern kibbutz of Ein Gev near the Sea of Galilee.

For the most part, Bashan is unlike the rest of Transjordan. It is a high country, with mountains rising ever higher to the east. In the north, dense foliage pushes back the desert compared to a narrow strip of cultivated land south of the Yarmuk River. Most of the Bashan gets rain or snow.

The Lower Golan (i.e., southern Bashan) starts at the eastern shore of Galilee, below sea level. Not far from the lake, barren hills rise steeply to a plateau about 400 m. (1,600 ft.) above the Sea of Galilee. In recent years, Syrian gunners trained their weapons on Israeli forces from that shelf. The Lower Golan held a prosperous Jewish community in New Testament times.

The Upper Golan is breath-taking, with exalted cone-shaped peaks and craters of extinct volcanoes. Erosion of the basalt soil has made a good grazing land. Less rain—3 to 3.5 cm. (12 to 14 inches)—falls on the plateau to the southeast, which was called Argob in the Old Testament. Moses reminded the Israelites that he led them to Bashan: "So the LORD our God delivered into our hands Og also, the king of Bashan, and all his people.... And we took all his cities at that time, there was not a city which we took not from them, threescore cities, all the region of Argob, the kingdom of Og in Bashan" (Deut. 3:3-4; cf. Deut. 3:13; 1 Kings 4:13; Num. 21:33).

Golan Heights. A scene of modern conflicts between the Israelis and Arabs, the Golan Heights is a tableland east-northeast of the Sea of Galilee. In Old Testament times it was part of the inheritance of Manasseh.

Hills of Gilead. Gilead was the hilly wooded country north of Heshbon and the Dead Sea. The hills flatten out into plains about 29 km. (18 mi.) south of Yarmuk and their northern extension forms the territory of Bashan. In its widest application the term Gilead can include all of Transjordan.

Still farther east is the Hauran, which Ezekiel included as part of the northeastern boundary of Israel (Ezek. 47:16, 18). The Hauran is jagged terrain, once having been the center of volcanic activity. Jebel Druz, the mountain of the Arabic-speaking Druze sect, pierces the sky at 1,500 m. (5,000 ft.). This rugged country made an ideal hide-out for robber bands, and later was a refuge for the persecuted Druze. Yet the area has enough moisture and good soil to grow crops.

Herod the Great took control of Bashan as early as 20 B.C., and left it to his son, Herod Philip, as an inheritance. Philip built up Caesarea Philippi as his capital, naming it in honor of the Caesar as well as himself. The province was given to Agrippa I in A.D. 37.

B. Gilead. The mountains of Gilead are an eastern counterpart to the hill country of Samaria, and the landscape, vegetation, and climate are somewhat similar. However, the eastern mountains rise higher: 1,000 to 1,200 m. (3,281 to 3,937 ft.) as compared with Mount Hebron's 990 m. (3,300 ft.). They also receive more rainfall, 75 cm. (30 in.) per year, instead of the 50 cm. (20 in.) per annum of Palestine.

A person who visits Gilead after being in Palestine is usually surprised at the many springs, villages, and shrub-covered hillsides. The visitor might also be surprised to learn that the famous "balm of Gilead" was not just a spiritual cure for the sin-sick soul. The ancient people used to export the "balm of Gilead"—probably tiny balls of sap from slashed evergreen trees—used for medicinal purposes. Joseph was sold to a caravan from Gilead, on its way to Egypt with "camels bearing spicery and balm and myrrh" (Gen. 37:25).

Gilead is an oval dome roughly split in two by the Jabbok River. The half-tribe of Manasseh settled northern Gilead, which was covered with thick brushwood and oaks. The more mountainous southern Gilead was allocated to Reuben. The high amount of precipitation, plus heavy dew in summer, produced lush growth. Year-round tributaries of the Yarmuk and Jordan rivers drained the excess water.

Several judges of Israel were natives of Gilead. Jair ruled Israel for 22 years from Camon, his home in northern Gilead. The judge Jephthah was the son of Gilead, but his mother was a harlot, so his step-brothers refused him a share of the inheritance. He fled to the land of Tob, where he formed a band of raiders. Later his brothers recalled his prowess as a warrior, and promised him the leadership of Gilead if he would lead their army against the Ammonites. Jephthah's forces attacked and defeated the Ammonites (Judg. 11:32).

For the most part, the Ammonites left the Israelites alone until the days of Saul. As Saul was about to assume the reign of Israel, an unsavory character named Nahash besieged the city of Jabesh-gilead. The inhabitants offered to serve him under a treaty, but he would agree only if they allowed him to gouge out their eyes! And Saul gathered the forces of Judah and Samaria to go to their rescue (1 Sam. 11:1-11). The people of Jabesh-gilead never forgot this act of kindness: "And when the inhabitants of Jabesh-gilead heard of that which the Philistines had done to Saul; All the valiant men arose, and went all night, and took the body of Saul and the bodies of his sons from the wall of Beth-shan, and came to Jabesh and burnt them there. And they took their bones, and buried them under a tree at Jabesh, and fasted seven days" (1 Sam. 31:11-13).

Elijah the prophet also came from Gilead (1 Kings 17:1), bringing God's word to Israel's King Ahab. During a three-year famine, he stayed by the brook Cherith in Gilead, where the water refreshed him and ravens brought food (1 Kings 17:3ff.). When his earthly ministry was finished, Elijah again crossed the Jordan into Gilead, where God's chariots snatched him up in a whirlwind (2 Kings 2:8ff.).

C. Perea. Looking at a map of the New Testament era, we

would see the names *Perea* and *Decapolis* on the area of Gilead. Decapolis was roughly equivalent to northern Gilead. Multitudes followed Jesus from this region, which extended to both sides of the Jordan River (Matt. 4:25).

"Beyond the Jordan" referred to Perea, a province bordering the Jordan River on the southeast. This was the territory of Herod Antipas, who had John the Baptist beheaded (Mark 6:14-29).

It was customary for Jews to avoid Samaria, so on His way to Jerusalem, Jesus generally crossed the Jordan to Perea. Opposite Jericho He crossed back over by fording the Jordan or taking a ferry, then continued His journey through the Judean wilderness to Jerusalem.

D. Ammon. Ammon is a vast grassland between the desert on the east and the green mountains of Gilead on the west. The mountains level off into a plateau, and since Ammon has no high mountains, there is little rainfall. But at Rabbah, "the city of waters" (2 Sam. 12:27), springs gush forth to make the beginnings of the Jabbok River. The well-watered areas of Ammon could be cultivated, but it was best suited for pasture. Ezekiel once prophesied that Rabbah would become "a stable for camels, and the Ammonites a couching place for flocks" (Ezek. 25:5).

E. Moab. Moab was another high pastureland. The 3,000-foot plateau bordering the Dead Sea between the Arnon and Zered rivers was partially planted in wheat and barley. Moab's King Mesha was a sheep breeder who paid a large tribute to King Ahab of Israel. After years of this, he rebelled against Ahab's successor, Jehoram (2 Kings 3:4-5).

The cities just north of the Arnon River—Dibon (modern Dhiban) and Aroer—were Moab's outposts. But the Moabites wanted the northern tableland of Heshbon and Medeba. Moses told of a time when Sihon, king of Heshbon, had pushed the Moabites back to the Arnon: "For there is a fire gone out of Heshbon, a flame from the city of Sihon: it hath consumed Ar of Moab, and the lords of the high places of Arnon. Woe to thee, Moab!" (Num. 21:28-29).

Eventually God gave Sihon's power into Israel's hand. When King Balak of Moab saw what had become of Sihon's Amorites, he panicked at the sight of the Israelites encamped below him in the plains of Moab. He sent for the diviner Balaam to come and curse the Israelites on his behalf, saying, "I wot that he whom you blessest is blessed, and he whom thou cursest is cursed" (Num. 22:6). But God told Balaam, "Thou shalt not curse the people: for they are blessed" (Num. 22:12). Though Balak was furious with Balaam for not doing as he asked, the invasion he feared did not come. Instead the Israelites settled down at Shittim and got into trouble by being overly friendly with the Moabites (Num. 25:1-2).

In the days of the judges, a famine in Judah caused Elimelech and Naomi and their sons to sojourn in Moab (Ruth 1:1). The sons married Moabite women. After their husbands died, Naomi and her daughter-in-law, Ruth, returned to Bethlehem, Naomi's former home. Ruth then married Boaz and became the great-grandmother of King David.

Both the Ammonites and the Moabites coveted the fertile Jordan Valley. When the Israelites conquered the kingdoms of Sihon and Og, the Ammonites and Moabites retreated to the safety of their borders. But each time one nation weakened, another would try to expand. Thus Israel, Ammon, and Moab were a constant threat to each other.

The Ammonites and Moabites pressed hard on the Israelites during the period of the judges. Eglon of Moab penetrated beyond the Jordan as far as Jericho (Judg. 3:12-14). Later, when Israel sinned, the Lord "sold them into...the hands of the children of Ammon" (Judg. 10:7), who oppressed both the Israelites in Gilead

Petra's Architecture. The rose-red city of Petra is one of the most unusual sites in the territory of Edom. This Nabataean town was carved from sheer sandstone rock cliffs around 300 B.C. The photograph shows a detail from the Petran structure which local Arabs call El Deir Monastery.

and those west of the Jordan—in Judah, Benjamin, and Ephraim.

King David turned the tables on the Ammonites, forcing them to work for him (2 Sam. 12:29-31). The Ammonites escaped the conquering Babylonians in 586 B.C., and they gloated as Judah was exiled to Babylonia (Ezek. 25:6). Time did not lessen the ancient animosity. When the Jews returned from exile and started to re-build the walls of Jerusalem, Ammonites showed up to taunt the workmen (Neh. 4:1-9). The Tobiad family ruled the Ammonites from the fifth to the second century B.C., and they never did learn to like the Jews.

F. Edom. Edom was another name for Esau, son of Isaac and brother of Jacob (Gen. 25:30; cf. 32:3). Originally Esau went to live in the hills of Seir, southeast of the Dead Sea. The area came to be known by his name, and the people were called Edomites.

Edom also means "red," and speaks of the reddish color of the sandstone mountains in south Edom. Here we find Petra, the fabled "red-rose city." In the time of Christ, the Nabataeans built the impenetrable fortress of Sela there, carving it from sandstone rocks. Visitors can see how these ancient people used the natural rocks of Edom for their protection. A narrow passage of steep rocks leads into Petra, and many of the caves they hollowed out and ornately decorated are well-preserved to this day.

The stark and imposing mountains of Edom are a radical change from the northern edge of Edom territory, the valley of Zered, as well as from the northern stretch of the King's Highway crossing the tableland of Moab. In Bible times, the northern cities of Tophel and Bozrah had more abundant vegetation. Their wood was sent south to make charcoal for the copper smelters at Punon. Even today the village of Tofileh (Tophel) harvests fine olive groves.

The peaks of south Edom exceed 1,500 m. (5,000 ft.)—a composite of sandstone, basalt, and crystalline rocks. The 45 to 50 cm. (16 to 20 in.) of yearly precipitation sometimes includes snow. The resulting vegetation encouraged people to settle there in biblical times.

Edom and Judah contended fiercely for control of a very important highway junction near the port of Ezion-geber. Here the King's Highway from the northeast met the road to Egypt across the Sinai, and a third highway took caravans farther south, to

Tema. Edom's economy hinged on access to this junction, but it was also valuable to Israel. Therefore the Israelites fought numerous battles attempting to subjugate Edom, Ammon, and Moab.

David did manage to conquer Edom (2 Sam. 8:13-14). Solomon extracted tribute from the Edomites, and they did not endanger his shipping ventures at Ezion-geber. But soon after Solomon's death they rebelled and shipping became unsafe. Later, King Jehoshaphat of Judah tried to send ships to Ophir for gold, but the ships were wrecked at Ezion-geber (1 Kings 22:48).

In further strife between the two peoples, the Edomites got the upper hand over Judah's King Jehoram (2 Kings 8:24) and King Ahaz (2 Kings 16:5-18). God may have permitted these nations to threaten Israel in order to force His people to depend on Him. With God's help, Israel would prosper and limit the conquests of her eastern neighbors.

THE WEATHER AND CLIMATE OF PALESTINE

How could Palestine have been called a land of milk and honey? Its eroded hills and stony deserts seem to suggest not abundance but hardship and deprivation. Could it be that in biblical times the land was blessed with more rainfall than now? Did a different climate cause a less eroded land to yield a greater bounty for those who loved and worked it?

The answer is that weather and climate today are essentially unchanged from biblical times. Bible descriptions of the early and latter rains, the heat of the day and the cool of the day are accurate; they might have been written yesterday or last week. What we see and experience today, our spiritual forefathers felt and saw then.

A. Climate and Weather. By climate is meant the characteristic weather of a region over a long period of time. This includes the periodic deviations from the expected patterns. Weather is the condition and behavior of atmospheric pressure, winds, cloud cover, precipitation, and types of precipitation at a particular time and place. The climate is the aggregation of weather patterns. Changes of climate are measured in terms of thousands of years, while the weather changes day to day or even hour by hour. The Bible gives a good description of the climate of Palestine, including its droughts and cloudbursts, such as the one at the end of Elijah's predicted three years of drought (1 Kin. 18:41-46).

B. Factors That Determine Palestinian Climate.

1. Latitude. This is the distance from the equator, either below or above. Palestine lies about the same distance north of the equator as the state of Georgia. It is on the north edge of the subtropical zone, but the southward shift of the zones in winter brings it within the temperate zone. Hence, it is a land of seasons.

2. Atmospheric movement. The global atmosphere moves constantly in currents and eddies, over Palestine as everywhere else. In summer the upper air moves sluggishly from the east, creating no storms. But as autumn comes, the winter season air pushes into the Mediterranean basin, clashes with tropical air masses, and creates eddies of low pressure. Storms of wind and rain are born. Ahead, the air is warm; behind these masses, it is cold. Sometimes in the winter season, cold dry air from Asia crosses the mountain barriers and sweeps across the land.

3. Large bodies of water. Palestine again is on the margin between one and the other. It has both a maritime and a continental climate. Warm moist air covers the coastline in summer, turning to rain in the winter. But the rains do not penetrate far inland. The double range of mountains lying across their path captures most of their moisture.

4. Topography. As mentioned above, the highlands steal water from passing clouds. The highlands run from north to south directly across the pathway of the moisture carriers. The abrupt changes in altitude from the highlands to the Rift or Jordan Valley dries and warms the clouds even further. The result is striking changes in climate within a few miles. Annual rainfall at Jerusalem is about 26 inches while fifteen miles east at the Dead Sea it is less than three and one-half inches. Temperature at the Dead Sea is fifteen degrees Fahrenheit higher than in Jerusalem.

C. The Climatic Regions of Palestine. Five definite climatic regions can be identified.

1. The coastal plain. Here between the Mediterranean and the nearby mountain ridges the influence of the sea dominates. Humidity is high and the annual range of temperature is less than in the hills.

2. The western highlands. This includes Mount Carmel. The

Moab and Edom. The land of Moab lay on the north (right) and the land of Edom to the south (left) of the Wadi Zered, which flows westward into the Dead Sea. The Edomites (descendants of Esau) inhabited a mountainous territory extending from the Zered to the Gulf of Aqaba. The descendants of Moab (a son of Lot) settled on the plateau east of the Dead Sea, between Wadi Zered and the Arnon River.

hilly plateau rises to a height of 3,000 feet, presenting a barrier to the prevailing easterly winds except where it is broken by the Plain of Esdraelon and the valleys of lower Galilee. The contours of the rainfall map follow closely the shape of the terrain.

3. The Rift Valley. This valley, in reality a gash in the earth's surface, embraces the Sea of Galilee, the Jordan River, and the Dead Sea. The Rift extends on through the Arabah and beyond into the continent of Africa. From above the Sea of Galilee, this valley is below sea level. The air which gave up its moisture to the western slopes is warmed and dried as it descends into the valley.

4. The plateau of Transjordan. Beyond the Rift Valley, this plateau in places is higher than the western ridges. These heights wring even more moisture from the atmosphere.

5. The deserts. The lower Rift Valley, the Negeb or southland, and the surrounding hills of Judea mark the southern boundaries of Palestine. Here are the subtropical deserts. They receive little rainfall; their only storms are whirlwinds and driving gales of dust and sand.

D. The Seasons. In reality Palestine has only two seasons, summer and winter. The periods between, spring and fall, are simply transitional.

Summer. The long, rainless summer begins in May or June and lasts through September, a season of consistently fine weather. There are regular winds and daytime heat but almost no rainfall. The average maximum temperature at Tel Aviv on the coast in August is 88 degrees Fahrenheit. In the central hill country average maximum temperature is 89 degrees Fahrenheit, but in the Jordan Valley, at Jericho, it is 99. The "cool" of the day comes as the sea breeze moves in beneath the rising warm air. This breeze reaches Jerusalem by noon, Jericho soon afterward, and the Jordan Valley by midafternoon. While rain is rare in June and almost never falls in July or August, the Mediterranean winds do carry moisture which they yield as generous dew nearly every morning. This eases the summer's grudging gifts of water.

Winter. Winter brings the rains, not continuous rains but alternating with bright periods. Sometimes they last one day, sometimes two. They are irregular but also dependable; they always come. For the farmer, everything depends on these rains.

After the onset of the rains in October there may be a pause, but then the remaining winter months are wet. By March and certainly no later than April the rains taper off. This is the growing season.

Transitional months. There is no spring or fall in Palestine. The transitional months are those that lead into the rainy season and those during which the rains taper off. The early rains are those that mark the tapering off of the rainy season. After the beginning of the rains in October, there may be a pause before the winter rains set in. But this early rain is important; it helps loosen the soil to get it ready for planting. In April and May the rainy season is ending, but still the latter rains may come. These rains are important because this now is the growing season. A dry period in April or early May means small crops. When the latter rains come, they give promise of a bountiful harvest.

2

MINERALS AND GEMS OF PALESTINE

Bible writers tell us the Israelites found a wide variety of minerals and precious stones in the Promised Land. They used these resources for building, jewelry, and fine crafts. In fact, these minerals became vital to Israel's export business.

CONSTRUCTION MATERIALS

Building projects consumed the largest quantity of Israel's mineral resources, but we have no evidence that the Hebrews ran short of mineral supplies. They used the most easily available minerals for building.

A. Hewn Stone. Most Israelites lived in houses built of hewn stone. The prophet Amos tells us that even the wealthy preferred "houses of hewn stone" (Amos 5:11), and Solomon used stone for the temple of Jerusalem (1 Kings 5:17; 7:12). Many kinds of building stone were available in Palestine, but it seems that marble and cheaper grades of limestone were most popular. Even in New Testament times, stone was the most common building material in the Holy Land, and Peter referred to Christians as "lively stones" in the structure that Christ built (1 Pet. 2:4-5).

The patriarchs gathered field stones to erect monuments and altars of worship (Gen. 35:14; Josh. 4:4-7). These landmarks lasted for many generations (cf. Gen. 35:20; Josh. 4:9).

True marble is a fine grade of limestone that will take a high polish. When the Bible refers to "marble," it most often means common limestone, which was more plentiful in Palestine. But in some cases it probably means true marble, as in God's plan for the temple (1 Chron. 29:2). Builders used different colors of marble to make mosaics and terrazzo floors, as in the palace of the Persian king at Shushan (Esther 1:6).

B. Bricks. Baked clay bricks were the Israelites' second favorite building material. The Bible first mentions brick in the construction of the Tower of Babel. There the builders said to one another, "Go to, let us make brick, and burn them thoroughly" (Gen. 11:3). So we think the builders baked their bricks in kilns, as the ancient Babylonians did. Archaeologists have found Babylonian bricks that were quite large, sometimes 30 cm. (about one foot) square, and flat. This shape could support the weight of large buildings better than today's rectangular bricks. Researchers think some of the early Israelite bricks may have followed this Babylonian pattern.

Clay was plentiful in Palestine, and the Hebrews used it for various jobs besides brickmaking; for example, they fashioned it into pottery and lamps. But the Hebrews molded clay bricks by the thousands, usually baking them in the sun. The bricks did not last as long as hewn stone. To make clay bricks more durable, kings and wealthy householders hardened them in charcoal-fired kilns (cf. Nah. 3:14). The Book of Exodus tells us how the Egyptians forced their Hebrew slaves to make bricks for the pharaoh (Exod. 5:6-7). No doubt the Hebrews taught this skill to their descendants, who entered the Promised Land.

C. Mortar and Plaster. The Hebrews often used "pitch" as mortar for their stone work. Pitch was asphalt, which the Hebrews dug from tar pits around the Dead Sea. The Bible also calls soft asphalt "slime" (Gen. 14:10). "Pitch" or "slime" exposed to the air for several days hardened to form a tight, resilient bond between the stones of Hebrew buildings. The Israelites also used pitch to seal their boats and fuel their torches (cf. Gen. 6:14; Exod. 2:3). The Egyptians used it to coat the linen wrappings of embalmed corpses, in order to keep out moisture.

The Israelites burned limestone, shells, and other materials to make lime for brick mortar. Isaiah said the wicked would be "as the burnings of lime" (Isa. 33:12), and Amos tells us that the Moabites "burned the bones of the king of Edom into lime" (Amos 2:1). So we are sure the ancients understood how to make lime. They mixed lime with clay and other materials to make a simple form of mortar. When they mixed these ingredients poorly, their "untempered mortar" crumbled very quickly (cf. Ezek. 13:10-11).

Sand was not as plentiful for the ancients as we might suppose. Most of Palestine was covered with coarse gravel and dust; sand was found only along riverbanks and the seacoast—but the Philistines controlled most of the coast. Yet the Israelites dredged sand from the Kishon River near Accho and other sites to make mortar, glass, and other products.

METALS

The Bible names only six metals as known to the Israelites: gold, silver, iron, lead, tin, and copper (also called "steel"). Although archaeologists have uncovered a wide variety of metal objects in Palestine, we have little evidence of mining operations there. Palestinians probably found metal ore along riverbeds and exposed areas of rock, or dug shallow trenches where metal-bearing miner-

Brick Making. The Israelites probably made bricks much the same way as the worker shown here. A wooden frame is still used to form the wet clay into a brick, which is then dried in the sun. Scholars believe that some Israelites dried their bricks in kilns.

als lay near the surface. The Israelites traded precious metals for farm products and other goods.

A. Gold. Gold was the heaviest metal known to the Israelites, and the easiest to shape into intricate artistic designs. The Egyptians had large quantities of gold. Classical historian Walafrid Strabo (A.D. 808–849) noted that the Nabataeans, who inhabited Moab and Edom, mined gold along the Sinai peninsula. The Bible says the Israelites bought gold from Ophir and Parvaim (which may have been in India—1 Chron. 29:4; 2 Chron. 3:6), as well as from Sheba and Raamah, which were probably on the southern coast of Arabia (Ezek. 27:22).

Despite being scarce, gold was widely used in building Solomon's Temple (1 Kings 7:48-50), in decorating the homes of the kings (1 Kings 10:17-22), and in making jewelry. Gold displayed its owner's prestige or royal power (Dan. 5:29; James 2:2).

Gold ore usually has impurities of other metals, which lend their characteristic color (e.g., copper impurities make yellow gold). Metal workers in biblical times did not know how to remove these impurities, so they tested gold by rubbing it across a black stone called a *touchstone* and observing the color of its mark. Zechariah suggests this when he describes how God will test His people (Zech. 13:9).

B. Silver. The Israelites imported silver from several countries, but most of it came from "Tarshish"—possibly the town of Tartessus in southern Spain (1 Kings 10:22; 2 Chron. 9:21). Amazing as it seems, the Bible says King Solomon imported so much silver for the temple project that he "made silver to be in Jerusalem as stones" (1 Kings 10:27), and he refused to make any of his drinking cups of silver because "it was nothing accounted of" (1 Kings 10:21)!

Because silver does not combine easily with other metals, it is easy to recognize in its natural state. Even the patriarchs prized it as a valuable commodity, and Genesis says that "Abram was very rich in cattle, in silver, and in gold" (Gen. 13:2). The Israelites used silver to decorate the tabernacle and the temple (Exod. 26:19; 1 Chron. 28:14-17), to make trumpets (Num. 10:2), and to make idols in their decadent days (Isa. 40:19).

Merchants carried silver pieces as a common medium of trade; as a matter of fact, the Old Testament often used the Hebrew word

Gold Helmet. Hammered from the single piece of metal, this gold helmet (twenty-fifth century B.C.) was found in a tomb in Ur. Fragments of cloth and wool stuffing suggest that the helmet was fitted with a quilted cap for comfort. The inner cap was probably held in place by laces threaded through the small holes around the rim of the helmet.

for silver (*keseph*) to mean "money." Even in Abraham's day, the value of property was determined in silver (Gen. 23:15-16). However, Israel did not make silver coins until after the Exile; early traders simply used standard bits of silver.

C. Iron. This was the most plentiful of the heavy metals the Hebrews learned to use. Genesis 4:22 says that Tubal-cain was the "instructor of every artificer in brass and iron," so iron was being used even before the age of the patriarchs. The Hebrew word for iron was *barzel*.

Scripture emphasizes the abundance of iron ore in Palestine, where the "stones are iron" (Deut. 8:9). Jeremiah suggests that the "northern iron"—perhaps from the mountains of Lebanon— was stronger than the iron from other regions of the Near East (Jer. 15:12).

We know the Israelites had iron tools when they entered Canaan, for God instructed them not to use iron instruments to build the altar of the tabernacle (Deut. 27:5). They made iron axe heads (2 Kings 6:5-6), spear tips (1 Sam. 17:7), harrows (2 Sam. 12:31), and other tools and weapons. Iron technology gave the Israelites' enemies an advantage in war. The Israelites complained to Joshua that "all the Canaanites that dwell in the land of the valley have chariots of iron" (Josh. 17:16). The Israelites rapidly mastered skills with iron, but did not learn how to make steel. When the King James Version mentions "steel," it means bronze, an alloy of copper and tin (e.g., Psa. 18:34).

D. Lead. This heavy white metal was familiar to the people of Old Testament days. They used it to purify silver in crude furnaces (Jer. 6:29) and to strengthen alloys of other metals (Ezek 22:20). When Job wished that his works "were graven with an iron pen and lead in the rock forever!" (Job 19:24), he referred to the practice of pouring molten lead into inscriptions in rock, to make them more easily readable. The Egyptians believed this metal had mystical powers, so they sometimes buried an embalmed corpse with a plate of lead on its chest.

E. Tin. Archaeologists have discovered many objects made of bronze scattered across the Near Eastern world. However, only small amounts of tin ore, used to make this alloy, were available in the Near East. The best supplies of tin ore were in Britain, Spain, and India. Ezekiel 27:12 tells us the Israelites got their tin from Tarshish; Tarshish may in turn have gotten its tin from Britain.

The Hebrews used tin in Moses' time (Num. 31:22). They

Minerals in the Dead Sea

The sparkling blue waters of the Dead Sea contain a high concentration of minerals. Rivers and streams flowing over the land near the Dead Sea dissolve salts from the soil and deposit them into the sea. The fresh water evaporates, leaving the chemicals in the sea and making it the saltiest body of water on earth. The Dead Sea concentration of mineral salts is nine times saltier than that of the oceans.

The minerals in the Dead Sea include the chlorides of sodium (salt), magnesium, potassium, calcium, and magnesium bromide. The presence of bituminous material in the sea has been known since ancient times. These lumps of bitumen, found floating on the surface, provide evidence of petroleum springs in the sea bed.

Ancient Hebrews enjoyed an unlimited supply of salt. They formed brine pits called "salt-pans" along the Dead Sea's flat coastal area. The sun evaporated the water in the pits, leaving behind an abundant supply of mineral salts.

Salt was the chief economic product of the ancient world, and the Hebrews used it in a variety of ways: for flavoring foods, preserving fish, curing meat, and pickling olives and vegetables. Salt was an ingredient in the sacred anointing oil and ritual sacrifices. Infants were rubbed in salt to insure good health before swaddling (Ezek. 16:4). Salt was believed to have been an antidote for tooth decay and was considered a treatment for toothache. The modern Jewish custom of laying meat in salt, to drain it of blood, was no doubt observed in Bible times. The use of salt in every sacrifice symbolized God's perpetual covenant with Israel (Num. 18:19).

Modern Israelis extract large amounts of mineral resources from the Dead Sea. A network of dikes form shallow pools over 100 sq. km. (40. sq. mi.) of the sea. As the temperature in the area sometimes rises to 125° F, the water evaporates, leaving chemical salts that are manufactured into potash for fertilizer and magnesium bromide for drugs, ethyl gasoline, and many other products.

called it *bedhit*. The prophets knew of the process of smelting tin with other metals to make strong alloys (Ezek. 22:20).

F. Copper. Ezra tells us that this versatile metal was "precious as gold" when the Israelites returned from the Exile (Ezra 8:27). Copper was used to make brass and bronze and was known in the biblical world as early as the time of Tubal-cain (Gen. 4:22).

The Hebrew word for copper was *nechosheth*. The KJV sometimes translates this word as "brass" when copper is clearly meant, as when God promised to lead His people into Canaan, "out of whose hills thou mayest dig brass" (Deut. 8:9).

Although the Israelites had a good supply of copper ore, they did not master the skills of refining it and shaping it. Thus, Solomon had to depend on Phoenician craftsmen to make copper furnishings for the temple (1 Kings 7:14ff.).

GEMS AND PRECIOUS STONES

The Israelites valued precious stones much as we do today. The Bible often links precious stones with the architecture of the temple (2 Chron. 3:6; 9:10), and John saw the heavenly Jerusalem "garnished" with them (Rev. 21:19).

Jewelers of Bible times used vague terms to describe their stones, and this causes some confusion. They might call any hard stone an "adamant," and any clear stone "crystal." They might switch the names of stones with similar colors. Or they might use names we no longer understand. So when we study the gems of the Bible, we must admit some mystery still shrouds the subject.

For example, Exodus 28:15-22 describes the breastplate worn by the high priest, which had four rows of precious stones. Each stone bore the name of one of the tribes of Israel, "like the engravings of a signet" (v. 21). Because the Israelites did not know how to engrave the hardest gems, it is doubtful whether the breastplate really held a diamond, sapphire, emerald, and topaz. We feel it is more likely these terms refer to softer stones, such as chalcedony, lapis lazuli, garnet, and chrysolite.

The Bible mentions over twenty gems and precious stones, which we will discuss in alphabetical order:

A. Adamant. As we have already noted, this word refers to any number of hard gems. It comes from the negative form of the Greek word *damazo*, which means "to subdue" or "to crush"; so adamant signifies something that cannot be broken. The Hebrew word behind this is *shamir*, which literally means "a thorn." It is the same word Israelites used to denote a diamond.

Ezekiel said, "As an adamant harder than flint have I made thy forehead" (Ezek. 3:9). Zechariah said that his rebellious people "made their hearts [as hard] as an adamant stone" (Zech. 7:12). Clearly the adamant stood for toughness and hardness, even though we do not know what specific gem(s) it identifies.

B. Agate. The KJV uses this word to translate two Hebrew words—*cadcod* and *shebo*. The first word occurs in Isaiah 54:12 and Ezekiel 27:16, and it literally means "ruddy" or "reddish." German scholar Wilhelm Gesenius (1786–1842) believed it actually refers to the ruby, and most Bible interpreters follow this idea. The second word (*shebo*) occurs in Exodus 28:19 and 39:12, and it probably refers to the true agate.

This stone is a form of chalcedony, with stripes or layers in various shades of black, brown, or blue. It can be polished to a high gloss, making it a favorite decorative material of architects in biblical times. The second stone of the third row in the high priest's breastplate was an agate (Exod. 28:19).

C. Alabaster. This white mineral is easy to carve and polish, so Israelites used it to make beautiful jars and vases. Two varieties of alabaster are found in the Near East: one is a pure form of gypsum; the other a reddish marble. The first kind crumbles too easily to be used for carving. The second kind has colorful markings and is partially transparent, so it appeals to the eye.

Archaeologists have recovered alabaster jars from Greek, Kanan, Egyptian, and Assyrian ruins. Ancient traders often sealed costly perfume in an alabaster jar, allowing the scent to escape only gradually through the jar's porous shell over many years. Greek poet Theocritus (third century B.C.) reports that the merchants of Palestine used alabaster jars in the same way. This explains why Jesus' disciples rebuked the woman who broke an alabaster vessel of perfume and poured the perfume upon Jesus' head (Mark 14:3). The disciples felt the precious scent could have been sold for money to give to the poor. Shortly after Jesus' time, the Romans and Greeks called any thin-necked vial an *alabastron*, or "alabaster," because that was the familiar shape of alabaster perfume jars. Some Bible commentators believe that when the woman opened the jar over Jesus' head, she broke the neck of such a vial.

D. Amber. This is the fossilized resin of trees. Deep yellow or orange in color, amber could be polished to a high luster. Our English versions use this word to translate the Hebrew *hashmal*, which probably was some kind of metal. The Septuagint and the Latin Vulgate take *hashmal* to mean electrum, the shiny alloy of silver and gold. So when the Bible mentions "the color of amber" (Ezek. 1:4, 27; 8:2), it may mean a bright silvery hue, rather than the orange or yellow color we associate with amber.

E. Amethyst. Westerners know amethyst as a rare variety of quartz, a six-sided purple crystal that is hard enough to scratch

Copper Wands. About 80 copper wands were found in the "Cave of the Treasure" in 1961 at Nahal Mishmar in Palestine. These objects date from the end of the fourth millennium B.C. Copper ore was plentiful in Israel, although the Israelites did not learn to refine it until after the reign of Solomon. The word *brass* in the King James Version probably refers to copper, instead of the alloy developed at a later time.

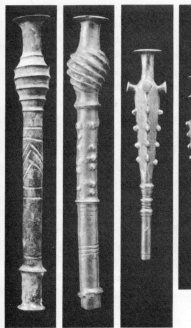

Breastplate of High Priest. This is a replica of the high priest's breastplate (cf. Exod. 28:15-21), which was set with stones representing the 12 tribes of Israel. The name of a tribe was engraved on each stone.

glass. But the people of the Near East are better acquainted with amethyst as a deep purple or violet form of corundum. The Hebrew word for it is *achlamah*, which may come from the stone's mythical ability to cause dreams (Hebrew, *halam*—"dream"). An amethyst was the third stone in the third row of the high priest's breastplate (Exod. 28:19), and John saw that the twelfth layer of the wall of the New Jerusalem was amethyst (Rev. 21:20).

F. Beryl. The Hebrew word for this stone was *tarshish*, perhaps because this gem was imported from the city of Tarshish. We know the beryl of biblical times as *aquamarine*; it is a yellow, green, or bluish crystal (depending on the chemical impurities in the gem). A beryl was the tenth stone in the fourth row of the high priest's breastplate (Exod. 28:20). The wheels of Ezekiel's vision and the man of Daniel's vision were the color of beryl (Ezek. 1:16; Dan. 10:6). Solomon and the King of Tyre wore jewelry of beryl (Song of Sol. 5:14; Ezek. 28:13).

G. Carbuncle. The KJV uses this word to translate two Hebrew words: *ekdāch*, which literally means "fiery glow," and *bārkath*, which means "flashing" or "sparking." Exodus 28:17 and 39:10 use carbuncle to name a jewel in the first row of the high priest's breastplate, but it may refer to any sparkling gem. The first word designates the deep red color we find in the true carbuncle. This word occurs in Isaiah 54:12, where the prophet describes the "gates of carbuncles" of the New Jerusalem.

H. Chrysolite. John says that the seventh foundation of the New Jerusalem was made of chrysolite—a golden yellow stone we feel may have been the same as the "beryl" of the Old Testament (Rev. 21:20). This stone was a yellow topaz or sardonyx.

I. Chrysoprasus. This grass-green gem formed the ninth foundation of the New Jerusalem in John's vision (Rev. 21:20). Mineral experts believe it was the same basic crystal as the chrysolite, but with nickel impurities that gave its greenish cast. The Septuagint stated that the Garden of Eden had gold, bdellium, and "chrysoprase" (Gen. 2:12); but later versions translate that word (*shoham*) as "onyx stone" or "beryl."

J. Coral. The merchants of Tyre sold coral to the wealthy people of Syria (Ezek. 27:16), who polished it for use in fine jewelry and inlaid work on buildings. Coral is the brilliant reddish or orange skeleton of sea animals, which forms reefs in the Mediterranean and other warm seas. It can be cut and polished like inorganic stone. The Old Testament uses two words for coral: *ramoth*, which refers to coral in a general sense (Ezek. 27:16), and *peninim*, which refers to red coral (Job 28:18).

K. Crystal. Rock crystal is a completely transparent form of quartz. The Hebrew word for crystal (*gerach*) also means "frost" or "ice." The ancients thought crystal was only ice congealed by intense cold. They valued it highly for its great beauty. Crystal's clarity is suggested in Revelation 4:6; 21:11; 22:1. Ezekiel describes the heavenly firmament as "the terrible crystal" (1:22). This mineral's beauty has given rise to such expressions as "clear as crystal."

L. Diamond. Diamond is pure crystallized charcoal or carbon. It is named as the third precious stone in the second row of the high priest's breastplate (Exod. 28:18; 39:11). But many scholars feel that this stone in the breastplate should have been translated as onyx, and that diamond was intended but the word translated *jasper* (e.g., Exod. 28:20).

In biblical times all diamonds were brought from India. The ancients supposed diamonds were indestructible in fire—but we now know this is not true. Jeremiah tells us the diamond was used as an instrument for engraving on hard materials (Jer. 17:1).

M. Emerald. This crystal stone owes its chief value to its deep green color. The emerald is named as the first stone in the second row of the high priest's breastplate (Exod. 28:18; 39:11). Many biblical scholars feel, however, that this stone should have been translated as "carbuncle." In any case, the ancients got emeralds from Cyprus, Egypt, and the mountains of Ethiopia. The emerald is mentioned in the description of the rainbow around God's throne (Rev. 4:3), and it makes up the fourth foundation of the walls of the heavenly Jerusalem (Rev. 21:19).

N. Jacinth. Biblical scholars have not had an easy time identifying this stone, which is mentioned in Revelation 21:20. Some historians consider it the same as amethyst; others link it with ligure (Exod. 28:19). Jacinth may have been a puce-red stone which came in brown and yellow varieties.

O. Jasper. Jasper is an opaque, impure variety of quartz that is mentioned in both the Old and New Testaments. Jasper comes in red, yellow, and some duller colors. When the colors are in stripes or bands, jasper is called striped quartz. As with a number of other precious stones mentioned in the Bible, scholars dispute whether modern jasper is meant in Scripture. But scholars agree that the Hebrew and Greek names (*yashpeh* and *iaspis*) have the same origin as our word *jasper*. Jasper was the third stone in the fourth row of Aaron's breastplate (Exod. 28:20). Revelation mentions jasper several times: He that sat upon the throne was "like a jasper and a sardine stone" (Rev. 4:3). (*See* "Sardine" below.) The light of the New Jerusalem appeared "like a jasper stone" (Rev. 21:11). And the first of the New Jerusalem's twelve foundations was jasper (Rev. 21:19).

P. Ligure. Modern scholars know of no stone with this name. Students of the Bible have very little idea what is meant by this stone, which was the first of the third row of precious stones on the breastplate of the high priest (Exod. 28:19; 39:12).

The Hebrew and Greek words for ligure (*leshem* and *ligurion*) suggest "to attract." Because amber has a magnetic attractive quality, some scholars think it is ligure. But this could not be so, because true amber is not a precious stone and is not hard enough for an engraver to work with. Therefore, it could not have been part of the high priest's breastplate.

Q. Onyx. Onyx is a type of agate stone with two or more colors in parallel bands or layers. The Hebrew word for onyx is *shoham*. The ancients found onyx in the land of Havilah (Gen. 2:12). Today onyx is a semiprecious stone, but in biblical times it was obviously of high value, since it is mentioned among precious stones and metals (Job 28:16; Ezek. 28:13). Onyx adorned the high priest's breastplate and two shoulders of his outer vestment (Exod. 28:9-12, 20).

R. Pearl. A pearl is a smooth, hard, white or bluish-gray growth formed inside the shell of some oysters and other mollusks. Usually roundish, the most valuable pearls are produced by the oyster species. In ancient times, pearls were used in the East as personal ornaments, as they are today (1 Tim. 2:9; Rev. 17:4; 18:12-16).

From the way pearls are mentioned in the New Testament, we know they were held among the most precious substances. Compared with gems, pearls were considered in biblical times even more valuable than today (Matt. 7:6; 13:45-46; Rev. 21:21).

S. Ruby. The ruby is a clear, deep red variety of corundum, a mineral second only to diamond in hardness. The price and value of wisdom has been likened to that of rubies (Job 28:18; Prov. 3:15; 8:11), and the value of a virtuous woman (Prov. 31:10).

T. Sapphire. This is a hard, clear deep blue type of corundum stone. The sapphire was one of the stones in the high priest's breastplate and in the foundation of the apocalyptic city (Exod. 28:18; Rev. 21:19).

The sapphire is often mentioned in the Old Testament. Sapphire is next to the diamond in luster, beauty, and hardness. Bible scholars generally agree, however, that the usual sapphire of biblical times is the same as our *lapis lazuli*, an opaque, dark blue mineral.

U. Sardine. We find the word *sardine* only in Revelation 4:3, where we are told that the Deity was like "a jasper and a sardine stone" to look upon. Most scholars feel it is the same stone referred to in the Old Testament under the Hebrew name of *ōdhem,* and the Septuagint as *sardion,* and the *sardius* of the Authorized Version.

Sardius is mentioned among the precious stones on the breastplate of the high priest (Exod. 28:17; 39:10) and is mentioned in connection with diamonds in Ezekiel 28:13. Sardine is a gem of blood-red or flesh color and may have a high polish. It got its name from Sardis, the capital city of ancient Lydia (modern Turkey), where it was first found. Sardine has long been a favorite of engravers, because it is very hard, yet easy to work with, and beautiful in color. Sardine comes under a variety of quartz called sarde.

V. Sardonyx. This stone is mentioned only in Revelation 21:20, where it is said to be the foundation of a wall. Sardonyx is a variety of chalcedony, a grayish or milky quartz. In this gem, a white opaque layer rests upon a clear red layer. Thus sardonyx combines the qualities of sarde and onyx—thus, its name.

W. Topaz. Scholars agree that topaz is the same as modern chrysolite, a soft and clear or translucent gem, usually pale green in color. A true topaz is usually clear with a yellowish tint, but may be brown, blue, green, or even colorless. The topaz was the second stone on the first row of the high priest's breastplate (Exod. 9:10; 28:17). The "topaz of Ethiopia" (Job 28:19) was known for its beauty and value.

OTHER MINERALS

The Bible also tells us of other minerals the Hebrews knew. We shall discuss them as a group because of their various uses.

A. Brimstone. The Hebrews used this term to describe any substance that caught fire easily, especially sulphur. We find brimstone mentioned in seven passages of the Old Testament (Gen. 19:24; Deut. 29:23; Job 18:15; Psa. 11:6; Isa. 30:33; 34:9; Ezek. 38:22).

Brimstone is also used as a symbol of God's fiery wrath and the future suffering of the wicked (Rev. 14:10; 19:20; 20:10; 21:8).

B. Flint. Flint is a very hard kind of quartz stone that produces sparks when struck against iron. It is usually brown, black, or gray. The Hebrews, like other ancient peoples, used flint to start fires for cooking and sacrifices. Flint was well-known and plentiful in Palestine and nearby districts (Psa. 114:8).

Bible writers also considered flint a symbol of things firm and constant (Isa. 50:7; Ezek. 3:9).

C. Nitre. This is an earthly alkaline salt that resembles soap. Indeed, the Hebrews often used it as soap. Nitre separated from the bottom of the Natron Lakes in Egypt and rose to the top, where it was condensed by the heat of the sun into a dry, hard substance like soap. Nitre is found in many other parts of the East.

Nitre is our translation of the Hebrew word *nether*. Vinegar has no effect on common nitre, but vinegar does affect *natron*, or soda. Probably the English translation of the substance referred to in Proverbs 25:20 and Jeremiah 2:22 should have been *natron* instead of *nitre*.

D. Salt. Salt held a place of great importance in the primitive and simple society of the ancient Israelites. Job tells us that salt was used from the oldest times to flavor food (Job 6:6). Ancient man sacrificed to God food he found pleasant, so salt was included among these offerings (Ezek. 43:24). By biblical times, salt had become linked with health, hospitality, purity, and durability. Ezekiel

Alabaster Jar. Fashioned as a container for oil, this Egyptian vessel from the tomb of Tutankhamen (fourteenth century B.C.) consists of an inner shell and an outer shell carved with open-work designs and inscriptions. The Israelites frequently made jars and vases from alabaster, since it was easy to carve and polish. Alabaster jars were often used for costly perfumes, because its porous texture allowed the scent to escape slowly into a room.

tells us that in ancient times the Israelites rubbed newborn children with salt (Ezek. 16:4).

Later religious rites emphasized the cleansing property of salt. Salt came to stand for the most sacred and binding of obligations. God said of His covenant with the Israelites, "It is a covenant of salt for ever" (Num. 18:19). Second Chronicles relates that "the LORD God of Israel gave the kingdom over Israel to David for ever, even to him and to his sons by a covenant of salt" (2 Chron. 13:5). Jesus told His disciples they were "the salt of the earth" (Matt. 5:13). Paul linked salt with wisdom: "Let your speech be always with grace, seasoned with salt" (Col. 4:6).

Plants and crops cannot grow in land that has too much salt. The Bible also deals with this aspect of the mineral. When Abimelech took the city of Shechem, we are told he sowed the land with salt, so that it would always remain barren and unfruitful (Judg. 9:45).

Salt was plentiful in Palestine. The famous Jebel Usdum is actually a mountain of rock salt, about 11 km. (7 mi.) long. This ridge extends along the south and southwest corners of the Dead Sea. Jews used rock salt from this ridge. They also got salt by evaporating the waters of the Mediterranean and Dead seas.

Bible critic Edward A. Robinson believes the large plain east of Jebel Usdum is the "valley of salt" where David's army defeated the Edomites (2 Sam. 8:13; 1 Chron. 18:12; 2 Chron. 25:11).

3

ANIMALS AND INSECTS
OF PALESTINE

"And God made the beast of the earth after his kind, and cattle after their kind, and every thing that creepeth upon the earth after his kind: and God saw that it was good" (Gen. 1:25).

From the creation account in Genesis to the symbolic beasts of Revelation, the Bible abounds with animals of every description. God paraded the animals before the first man, so Adam could name them (Gen. 2:19-20). When Adam and Eve discovered their nakedness, God clothed them with animal skins. Throughout history animals have been an integral part of mankind's existence. They provided food as well as clothing, carried his burdens, drew his plow. They even spilled their blood for his sins.

The biblical writers were not naturalists, but many had keen eyes. The prophet Habakkuk watched the sure-footed deer nimbly pick their way across the treacherous rocks of the Judean hills. Then he exulted, "The LORD God is my strength, and he will make my feet like hinds' feet, and he will make me to walk upon mine high places" (Hab. 3:19). Others taught lessons by comparing the natures of beast and man.

About 80 mammals are named in Scripture. And that is not a complete list of the animals which live in the little land of Palestine. Sometimes we read and wonder. Are there really such things as unicorns, satyrs, dragons? What on earth is—or was—Behemoth? Leviathan? Did lions and bears really prowl the Holy Land? What of such strange-sounding beasts as the chamois or pygarg? The Bible mentions everyday animals too—cattle and horses, sheep and goats. Did puppies and kittens amuse little children in biblical days?

IDENTIFYING THE ANIMALS

Not all of these questions have answers. Some of the animal knowledge has been lost or distorted in transmission. Thus various translations of the Bible differ considerably in animal identification. Take a verse like Exodus 25:5 or Isaiah 34:14 and trace it through several Bible translations. For example, in the Exodus passage badgers' skins in the King James Version become goatskins in the Revised Standard Version. This is only one of the changes you will find.

We must remember that the KJV was written in the 1600s. At that time most people believed that unicorns and satyrs and dragons, for instance, were real. Now we know that they were imaginary beasts that came into our language through Greek and Roman myths. Such fanciful beasts are rarely mentioned in modern translations. "Unicorn" is generally replaced by "wild ox," as in Job 39:9 (RSV): "Is the wild ox willing to serve you?" One of the earliest translations, the Vulgate, called it a rhinoceros. Though the Hebrew term (*reem*) appears several times, only Psalm 92:10 indicates an animal with a single horn.

Satyrs are still found in the RSV of 1952. But the Hebrew term is translated "devils" in other verses, and "he-goats" in other versions. The mythical satyr is half-man, half-goat. That image fits easily into Isaiah's prophecy of desolation: "But wild beasts of the desert shall lie there; and their houses shall be full of doleful creatures; and owls shall dwell there, and satyrs shall dance there" (Isa. 13:21; cf. 34:14).

You can find a real dragon in the encyclopedia, but it is only an overgrown lizard that neither flies nor spouts flames. You will also find the word "dragon" in most modern Bibles. However, it is used only in a symbolic sense. Where a literal animal was intended, as in Jeremiah 9:11, the Revised Standard Version substituted "a lair of jackals" for "a den of dragons." *Serpents* in the Revised Standard Version replaces *dragons* in Deuteronomy 32:33: "Their wine is the poison of dragons (serpents, RSV), and the cruel venom of asps."

Satyrs and unicorns lend color to the King James Version. For a precise rendering of the Hebrew terms for animals, however, we need to consult additional translations and study aids. Even that cannot insure total accuracy. Thousands of years have passed since some of these animals walked the earth. During that period both languages and the distribution of animals have undergone changes. Some species are even extinct.

Yet, we are intrigued by the mysterious creatures of the Bible. Even today scholars disagree on the meaning of *behemoth* and *leviathan* (Job 40:15-24; 41). Some think these words referred not to real animals, but to mythological beasts, larger than life—as we speak of "monsters." Others think the behemoth was an elephant or a hippopotamus, and the leviathan was a crocodile. On the other hand, the New English Bible translates *behemoth* as "crocodile" and *leviathan* as "whale"! We can see how they reach such divergent conclusions. The verses in Job, though strikingly detailed, could apply to more than one animal. "He moveth his tail like a cedar" (Job 40:17), for instance, could be said of either an elephant or a crocodile. "He drinketh up a river" (Job 40:23)

Animals on Pottery. Cattle and various birds decorate these pieces of pottery from the sixteenth century B.C., found at Tell Ajjul in Palestine.

sounds very much like an elephant. But a hippo's home is the river, and he may appear to consume it as he submerges. Elephants and hippos were not unknown to the ancient Hebrews, and crocodiles once sunned themselves on the banks of the Jordan River.

Three continents converge at the Holy Land: Europe, Asia, and Africa. Animals from these areas have made their way into Palestine. Mountain sheep may have come from the island of Cyprus, gazelles from Africa, bears from Syria.

At times the Israelites lived in exile—as in Egypt or Persia. They became acquainted with the wildlife of those countries as well as the animals of their homeland.

As far back as King Solomon, exotic animals were imported. "Once in three years," according to 1 Kings 10:22, "came the navy of Tarshish, bringing gold, and silver, ivory, and apes, and peacocks." Such neighboring countries as Assyria had public zoos and even bred lions for the royal hunt.[1]

MAMMALS

The Hebrews found a prolific variety of mammals in the Promised Land itself. They domesticated many of these animals for agricultural power and other uses.

A. Domestic Animals. For the most part, the animals we read of in the Bible are the common animals, although not considered to be pets. Keeping animals solely as pets was a luxury the Israelites could not afford. The common animals of the Bible were what we would think of as farm animals—sheep and goats, cattle, beasts of burden.

1. Asses. The lowly ass—our donkey—was the conventional beast of burden. The Hebrew term *hamor* ("red animal") referred to the domestic ass. Able to subsist on very coarse food, this hardy creature also had multiple uses. The female (she-ass) was often ridden, and could be milked. Like the ox, the ass helped plow the fields and trample in the seed.

If you wanted to ride instead of walk, the ass was your most probable conveyance. Persons of rank, such as governors, could afford white asses (Judg. 5:10). The ass was a symbol of humility and patient service. Jesus entered Jerusalem as Zechariah foretold:

"Lo, your king comes to you; triumphant and victorious is he, humble and riding on an ass, on a colt the foal of an ass" (Zech. 9:9, RSV).

2. Camels. To the Hebrews, camels (*gamal*) were predominantly a beast of burden. Camels are bad-tempered, a bit dense, and complain when they have to carry a load. But God must have created the camel expressly for desert nomads. This animal is superbly engineered to cope with a hot harsh environment. Long legs keep the camel's belly comfortably away from the blazing sands. (A rider careens along about 2 m. [6.5 ft.] off the ground.) The camel conserves water admirably. Its thick wool coat provides natural insulation; it maintains an even body temperature and hardly perspires at all. Though a thirsty camel may gulp 105 l. (25 gal.) of water within ten minutes, he can go for long periods without food and even longer without water. The dromedary camel familiar to Bible writers had but one hump—his reserve fuel tank. It is not a hollow cistern of water, as some believe, but a mass of muscle and fat. After an arduous journey, the once-firm hump may be floppy and soft and have to be built up again.

Arabs prized the camel much as Israelites valued the goat. It supplied transportation, milk and meat, and clothing from its soft hair; even the dung chips were burned for fuel. Jews did not eat camel as the Arabs did, because camels were considered unclean (cf. Deut. 14:7). But rich men like Abraham and Job counted camels among their possessions (Gen 22:16; Job 1:3; 42:12). Jeremiah's comment, "Thou art a swift dromedary traversing her ways" (Jer. 2:23b), indicates that a dromedary camel was their equivalent of our racehorse. The dromedary could cover 13 to 16 km. (8 to 10 mi.) per hour.

The two-humped Bactrian camel of central Asia is probably the type of camel referred to in Isaiah 21:7.

3. Cats. Though there's no shortage of cats in modern Israel, they were practically unknown in ancient Mesopotamia. But they were worshiped in ancient Egypt, so cats may have entered the Palestinian scene at any time. The Bible does not mention them.

4. Cattle. The soft lowing of cattle was as familiar in Bible times as the baas of sheep and goats. Cows, calves, heifers, and bulls are mentioned, but the *ox* appears more frequently. *Oxen* are the adult cattle used as draft animals. With sheep and goats to supply meat and milk, Israelite farmers depended on oxen as modern farmers rely on tractors. Broken to service at three years, oxen pulled plows, threshed grain, and drew carts. The full-grown animals were regarded as too valuable for slaughter.

One had to be wealthy, as Abraham was, to keep many cattle (Gen. 12:16; 21:27). Being larger animals, they needed more and better pasture than goats or sheep. Some areas of Palestine were better for grazing herds—Bashan in the north and Gilead east of the Jordan. When pasture was scant, or an animal was to be eaten, cattle were penned and given fodder. The "stalled ox" of Proverbs 15:17 had been fattened up for the table.

In the Bible, "cattle" had the broader meaning of "livestock." Thus cattle included sheep and goats as well as asses, mules, horses, and even camels. This may explain why the tribes of Gad and Reuben proposed to "build sheepfolds...for our cattle" (Num. 32:16).

5. Dogs. Dogs had value as service animals and were domesticated quite early in history. Job spoke of "the dogs of my flock" (30:1). Some were trained as watchdogs. Greyhounds, described in Proverbs 30:30-31 as "comely in going," were used by kings for

Camels. The Hebrews used camels as beasts of burden. Bad-tempered though they are, camels are well-adapted to desert life. Their thick coats provide insulation against the extreme heat, and they can go for long periods without food and even longer without water. These camels are about to be sold at a camel market in Beer-sheba.

hunting. Many dogs were half-wild scavengers. They roamed the streets in search of food and would even consume human flesh. Queen Jezebel, you may recall, was thrown into the streets and her corpse was eaten by dogs (2 Kings 9:35-37).

"Dog" was a term of derision. In this symbolic sense it appears several times in Hebrew and Greek texts. "Dog" (Greek, *kuon*) stood for a false teacher (Phil. 3:2) or a sinner (Rev. 22:15). *Keleb*, the most common Hebrew term for dog, symbolized a persecutor of God's people (Psa. 22:16). Jesus spoke of casting food for the "children"—i.e., the Jews—to the non-Jews who were "dogs" (Greek, *kunarion*; Matt. 15:26). In later history, Muslims showed their contempt for Christians by calling them "dogs."

6. Goats. Goats, sometimes called "the poor man's cow," were also domesticated early. They did not need good pasture; they liked to eat bark and tender twigs. Goats were terribly hard on vegetation; they ate everything within reach, including fledgling trees and shrubs. Their excessive numbers and indiscriminate grazing have been blamed for some of the barren hills of present-day Israel.[2]

But to the Israelites in Bible times, goats had great value. They supplied milk and milk products. The meat tasted like venison; the young kids were especially tender. Goat hair was not shorn, but combed from the animals and woven into coarse cloth. (Curtains of the tabernacle were made of goats' hair—Exod. 26:7.) Goatskin made good leather and water bottles. Even the horns of rams were used for drinking vessels and musical instruments. A man with a large flock of goats was indeed well off. By careful breeding of his flocks, Jacob became a rich man (Gen. 30).

Goats had their drawbacks—they stank, and they were lively, strong-willed creatures, unlike their docile cousins the sheep. In Jesus' parable, when the sheep and goats were separated, the goats wound up on the left, a position of disfavor (Matt. 25:32-33).

7. Horses. Horses were also latecomers to Israel and never did attain a position of great importance. They were used by the Egyptians and Assyrians for warfare, but Israel's king was told not to "multiply horses to himself, nor cause the people to return to Egypt, to the end that he should multiply horses..." (Deut. 17:16). Isaiah warned, "Woe to them that go down to Egypt for help; and stay on horses, and trust in chariots" (Isa. 31:1). Nevertheless, King Solomon "had a thousand and four hundred chariots, and twelve thousand horsemen, whom he bestowed in the cities for chariots, and with the king at Jerusalem" (1 Kings 10:26). He imported them from Egypt at a cost of 600 silver shekels per chariot and 150 shekels per horse (1 Kings 10:29). Even in the New Testament book of Revelation, horses are linked with war (Rev. 6:1-8).

As time passed, horses took their place as riding animals, along with the ass, mule, and camel. They even served in a primitive "pony express": "He...sent letters by posts on horseback" (Esther 8:10). But Psalm 32:9 expressed a disparaging view: "Be ye not as the horse, or as the mule, which have no understanding."

8. Mules. Mules (Hebrew, *pered*) were the hybrid offspring of a male ass and a female horse. They were stronger and more enduring than asses and more sure-footed and longer-lived than horses. Yet the Israelites were prohibited from mating ass and horse (Lev. 19:19). Mules were probably not used in Israel until the time of King David, and then were likely imported from Egypt. David's son Absalom was astride a mule when his head caught in the boughs of an oak, leaving him at the mercy of his enemies (2 Sam. 18:9).

9. Sheep. Sheep are mentioned about 750 times in Scripture, and are undoubtedly the most familiar biblical animal symbol.

Often flocks were mixed, goats and sheep grazing amicably together. Sheep were well-suited for a nomadic life, but they were very dependent on their shepherd. He led them to pasture, found water to quench their thirst, protected them from wild beasts. A good shepherd cared deeply for his sheep. He not only knew how many were in his flock, but could call them by name. The sheep in turn knew their shepherd's voice. Jesus illustrated God's tender concern for His children by comparing Himself to a good shepherd, willing even to lay down his life for his sheep (John 10:1-15).

"Keeper of sheep" was the first profession named in the Bible (Gen. 4:2). Throughout Israel's history shepherding continued to be a very respectable calling, although shepherds as a class were distrusted in Jesus' day, as being a wild lot. The beloved King David was once a shepherd boy. And unpretentious shepherds were the first to be told of the Messiah's arrival.

Sheep have not changed since Bible times. The broad-tailed

sheep was, and still is, prevalent in Israel. Some sheep had such fat tails that they pulled little wagons on which to rest them! The ewes were milked. Since sheep were considered to be clean (Deut. 14:6), mutton was an everyday meat.

The sheep's precious wool (often dark-colored) provided warm garments. Once a year the sheep were herded into an enclosure for shearing. Like the "husking bees" of the American farm heritage, sheep-shearing made a good excuse to socialize. Absalom killed his brother Amnon during the hubbub of one sheep-shearing (2 Sam. 13:23-29).

10. Swine. *See* "Boars."

B. Wild Animals. It is difficult to identify many of the wild animals mentioned in the Bible. Biblical writers may have referred to several species with one general term. In this section, we will attempt to distinguish between them by noting the various types of wild animals found in Palestine today.

1. Wild Asses. The wild ass of Syria (Hebrew, *peres*) is mentioned several times (Job 24:5; Psa. 104:11; Isa. 32:14). They were occasionally found in northern Palestine. Daniel 5:21 may refer to the larger species, which was common in Arabia.

2. Badgers. Although badger skins are mentioned several times in the King James Version, that is a disputable translation of the Hebrew. Exodus 26:14 states that craftsmen working on the tabernacle made "a covering for the tent of rams' skins dyed red, and a covering of badgers' skins." One naturalist makes a good case for retaining that interpretation.[3] The honey badger, he notes, ranges from Africa to India, and has a thick loose skin. Such a hide would be durable, suitable for weatherproofing the tabernacle. Since badgers are small animals, quite a quantity of their pelts would be needed. This would raise their value and explain their place among such listed treasures as gold and jewels.

However, later translators did away with badgers entirely. The New English Bible reads "porpoise hides" where badger skins were named in regard to the tabernacle. The RSV uses *goatskins*. *Leather* is substituted in Ezekiel 16:10: "I clothed you also with embroidered cloth and shod you with leather" (RSV). According to some authorities, the Hebrew term (*tachash*) translated *badger* designates not an animal but a color (black or blue). It may have referred to the tough skin of a marine animal, such as the dugong or even the whale, which can be found in the Red Sea. There is evidence that "porpoise hides" were highly prized by the other nations of antiquity.

3. Bears. Now found mostly in the mountains of Lebanon, the Syrian bear once roamed the entire area. This light-colored bear liked to prey on sheep and goats. A "bear robbed of her whelps" was a popular expression to indicate a state of uncontrollable rage. There are not many references to bears in Scripture, though they cropped up as symbols in visions given to Isaiah, Daniel, and John (Isa. 11:7; Dan. 7:5; Rev. 13:2).

4. Boars. The Israelites contended with wild boars from the Hula Valley all the way down to the desert near the Dead Sea. Boars were so damaging to crops that farmers sometimes had to set a watch for them. They were vicious when crossed by man and seemed to delight in trampling and destroying his carefully tended vineyards. The Psalmist compared the cruel ravishing of Israel by her enemies to a vine at the edge of a woods: "The boar out of the wood doth waste it" (Psa. 80:13).

Domestic swine were raised too, though pigs were abhorred throughout the Middle East, not only by the Jews. Yet someone, even in Bible days, kept pigs, for Christ cast demons into a herd of swine (Matt. 8:28-34). He mentioned them more than once in His teaching, always as a symbol of degradation, as in the story of the prodigal son (Luke 15:15). They were strictly forbidden as food. "Many will be slain by the Lord," Isaiah predicted direly, "those who eat the flesh of pigs and rats and all vile vermin" (66:17, RSV).

5. Coneys. The coney of the Bible is really a rock hyrax, which looks somewhat like a rabbit-sized guinea pig. Proverbs 30:26 states, "The coneys are but a feeble folk, yet make they their houses in the rocks." Hyraxes easily scramble about seemingly inaccessible terrain. Their feet have a built-in suction that gives them incredible clinging power on even the steepest rock surfaces.

6. Deer. After the Flood, wild animals became part of the food supply. God told Noah, "Every moving thing that liveth shall be meat for you" (Gen. 9:3).

Two types of deer are mentioned in the Bible, the fallow deer and the roe deer. (Males and females are not called bucks and does, but harts and hinds.) The true fallow deer (Hebrew, *yahmur*) are beautiful creatures, similar to North American deer. Deuteronomy 14:5 and 1 Kings 14:23 refer to this type.

The roe deer or roebuck was noted for its swiftness. In Song of Solomon 2:8-9, the young lover comes "leaping upon the mountains, skipping upon the hills" like a roe or a young hart.

Gazelle has replaced "roe deer" in many translations. These two animals closely resemble each other. The gazelle is buff-colored and fine-featured, with large liquid eyes and distinctive horns. In numerous biblical comparisons they exemplify beauty, affection, and agility (Song of Sol. 2:17; 8:14).

Deer hunting is an ancient sport. Esau was "a cunning hunter" (Gen. 25:27-28); the venison he brought home endeared him to his father Isaac. King Solomon's menu included "harts, and roebucks, and fallow deer" (1 Kings 4:23).

7. Foxes. Foxes were not dangerous, but they were destructive. The fox is a member of the dog family, with a sharp pointed nose

Lion and Dog Fighting. This relief was found in the fourteenth-century B.C. stratum at the tell of Beth-shean in Palestine. Above, a dog and a lion rise up on their hind legs to fight; below, the dog bites the rump of the standing lion.

and bushy tail. They are cunning hunters, eating small animals and birds and having a fondness for certain fruit. Song of Solomon 2:15 tells of "the little foxes, that spoil the vines." But they helped keep down the mouse population.

Foxes live alone or in pairs, but do not go in packs as jackals do. This explains a later version of Judges 15:4, which tells that Samson caught 300 jackals (KJV, "foxes") and sent them into the fields with firebrands tied between their tails. They live in holes or rocky caves, often secondhand burrows abandoned by other animals. Jesus pointed out that even foxes had holes, but He had not dwelling of His own (Matt. 8:20). He also tartly called King Herod a fox (Luke 13:32).

Two species of fox are now found in Palestine: the tawny fox and the Egyptian fox.

8. Wild Goats. There were goats everywhere in Palestine, both tame and wild. En-gedi (Spring of the Kid), an oasis near the Dead Sea, still teems with wild goats, particularly a breed now known as the Nubian ibex. "The high hills are a refuge for the wild goats," according to Psalm 104:18.

9. Hares, Ferrets, Weasels. This trio was mentioned only as forbidden for food (see Lev. 11:6, 29-30). Hares, which are plentiful in Palestine, appear to chew a cud because of a peculiar movement of their mouths. Thus they were considered unclean. But they are not true ruminants. The common hare of Palestine looks like a jumbo rabbit; but unlike baby rabbits, hares are born with a coat of hair and are able to see.

Ferrets are rat-catchers related to weasels. Later translators substituted a wall lizard, *gecko*, in the Levitical list.

Weasels (Hebrew, *haled*) exist in almost every part of the world. They are small furry animals with long slender bodies and short legs, adept at squeezing through small openings. They dine on small rodents, and like skunks can spray attackers with a foul odor. The weasel is found throughout Palestine.

10. Hyenas. The hyena is not mentioned in the King James Version. But hyenas do live in Palestine and may be among the "wild beasts" of such passages as Jeremiah 7:33: "And carcasses of this people shall be meat for the fowls of the heaven, and for the beasts of the earth." A hyena resembles a wolf, but is a dirty gray color with dark stripes. Hyenas are scavengers, despised by man.

They will even dig up and devour human corpses. They have such strong jaws that they can easily crack the bones of an ox. Though savage, they are rather cowardly when confronted by man.

11. Jackals. Jackals are not specified in the King James Version either. But they were probably meant in certain scriptures which mention dragons, such as Micah 1:8, and were probably the animal meant in some passages reading *foxes*. The Revised Standard Version reads: "For this will I lament and wail; I will go stripped and naked; I will make lamentation like the jackals." Until recent times the chorus of jackals was a familiar night noise in Palestine. They tended to travel in packs and inhabit deserted places. Isaiah refers to "the haunt of jackals" (34:13, RSV).

12. Leopards. Flocks, herds, and humans had to beware of leopards. "A leopard shall watch over their cities: every one that goeth out thence shall be torn in pieces" (Jer. 5:6). The leopard is intelligent and wary; it is a better fighter than a lion, and more savage. Leopards lived in the mountains of Carmel and Lebanon, as well as in the woody "jungle" near the Jordan.

The cheetah is a smaller version of the big spotted cat and is probably the beast meant in Habakkuk 1:8: "Their horses also are swifter than the leopards." Jeremiah doubted the likelihood of Israel's repentance, asking sardonically, "Can the Ethiopian change his skin, or the leopard his spots" (Jer. 13:23).

13. Lions. Fierce predators also stalked the hills and the thickets of Palestine. Lions, found in almost half the books of the Bible, were a very real danger. The biblical lion was smaller than the African lion and had a short curly mane, but was no less feared. Even thinking about "the roaring of the lion, and the voice of the fierce lion, and the teeth of the young lions" (Job 4:10-11) could send shivers down one's spine.

Though some brave souls killed lions in individual combat (Judg. 14:5-6), Ezekiel 19:1-9 tells of capturing lions in a pit with nets. Lion hunting was a favorite sport of Near Eastern kings. Darius of Persia was not eccentric in keeping a den of lions (cf. Dan. 6:16-23). Early Christians were thrown to the lions when Rome raged against the fledgling church.

Kings may have hunted lions for sport, but shepherds and common men killed them in self-protection. Lions had lairs in the thickets bordering the Jordan River. When rising flood waters

forced them out, they made irascible neighbors. Jeremiah anticipated the rising judgment of God: "He shall come up like a lion
from the swelling of Jordan" (Jer. 49:19).

Mentioned more than any other wild beast in the Bible, the lion
symbolized royalty, courage, and power. It was the symbol of the
tribes of Judah, Dan, and Gad. In Revelation 5:5, Jesus is referred
to as "the Lion of the tribe of Judah."

14. Mice. Some wild animals were pests. Mice were a common
scourge, especially in grain-growing areas. Twenty-three species of
mice consider the Promised Land their land too. They could be as
destructive as locusts, destroying grain as it sprouted in the fields.
When the Philistines captured the ark of the covenant, they were
afflicted with *buboes* (the characteristic lesion of the lice-borne plague) and mice. In restitution they had to make golden images of
both the tumors and of the "mice that mar the land" (1 Sam. 6:5).
The Israelites were not supposed to eat mice, but apparently some
did so (Isa. 66:17).

15. Moles. When *moles* appear in the Bible record, probably the
mole-rat is meant, since there are no true moles in Israel. Like our
gophers, mole-rats are the bane of farmers. They live underground and burrow tunnels that wreak havoc with gardens. Despite their silky silvery fur, the mole-rats are rather ugly little
beasts. No eyes, ears, or tail can be seen—just a pig-like snout and

Relief from Khorsabad.
This relief from the eighth
century B.C. was
discovered at the palace
of Sargon, king of
Assyria, at Khorsabad.
The Persians used horses
to maintain an efficient
postal system. King
Solomon had thousands
of horses for warfare.

beaver-like teeth. Isaiah foresaw a day when men would cast away their idols "to the moles and to the bats" (Isa. 2:20).

16. Pygarg, Chamois. Since these animals appear only in Moses' list of clean animals (Deut. 14:5), translators didn't have much to go on. "Pygarg" is replaced by "ibex" in later versions, suggesting a type of bearded wild goat.

King James Version translators were acquainted with the chamois, a goat-like antelope found in Europe's colder climate. But *zemer,* the original Hebrew term, probably refers to some kind of wild mountain sheep.

17. Wolves. Wolves were fierce, cruel enemies. Light-colored and resembling large dogs, wolves in Palestine traveled singly or in groups of three or four. They were a variety of the European wolf and are still found in Palestine. They were a particular threat to sheep. The tranquility of the Messiah's reign will indeed be miraculous when "the wolf also shall dwell with the lamb," as Isaiah 11:6 foretold.

The patriarch Jacob, foreseeing the warlike character of one son, predicted "Benjamin shall ravin as a wolf" (Gen. 49:27). Jesus used the wolf to warn of treachery: "Beware of false prophets, which come to you in sheep's clothing, but inwardly they are ravening wolves" (Matt. 7:15).

C. Mammals in Modern Israel. The passing years have reshaped the face of Palestine. Areas once wooded are now barren hills. Swamps where hippos wallowed have been drained and reclaimed for cropland. In the modern State of Israel, space is precious. Wild places are dwindling.

Gone are the bears and lions, the formidable crocodiles, even the wild asses. The fallow deer has not been seen in Israel in this century. Modernization has left little need for beasts of burden. But camels, mules, asses, and horses are still in evidence.

Sheep and goats still dot the landscape. The beef and dairy industries are thriving. Many common animals still live there: foxes, coneys, hares, mole-rats, and of course mice.

Two species very nearly disappeared from the area entirely, the Nubian ibex (wild goat) and the gazelle. However, the State of Israel instituted strict protective measures and they have been preserved. In fact, gazelles are now agricultural pests.

The wild boar is the largest game animal left in Israel. Wolves, hyenas, and leopards are protected; jackals are rare.

The people of Israel, along with thoughtful people the world over, are awakening to their serious responsibility for the animals God placed in their dominion. Modern Israelis are planting trees where forests once flourished, and they are attempting to reintroduce wildlife that had vanished. At the National Biblical Zoo in Jerusalem it is possible to see many types of animals mentioned in the Bible.

BIRDS AND FISH

The first chapter of Genesis tells us that God said, "Let the waters bring forth, abundantly the moving creature that hath life, and fowl that may fly above the earth in the open firmament of heaven" (Gen. 1:20). On the fifth day of creation, God "created great whales, and every living creature that moveth, which the waters brought forth abundantly, after their kind, and every winged fowl after his kind" (Gen. 1:22).

A. Birds. Birds were common in Palestine and the people of biblical times used them for many different purposes. (For example, they used the pigeon and dove for sacrifice when a lamb was unavailable.)

Bible writers often used bird symbols to describe man's spiritual condition. For example, the church is compared to a "turtledove" (Psa. 74:19), as being gentle and vulnerable. Again, the writers of Scripture were fascinated by the magnificence of the eagle and its ability to soar in the sky. For this reason, they used the symbol of the eagle to challenge man to rise above his circumstances and follow God (cf. Prov. 23:5).

The Jewish law code forbade anyone to kill a mother bird, though a hunter could take her young (Deut. 22:6-7). The hunters usually caught their prey with a snare.

God's law divided birds into clean and unclean categories, like the other animals. The distinction was made on the basis of a bird's diet. Unclean birds were those that ate flesh, while clean birds were those that ate grain or seeds (Lev. 11:13-21).

Sheep. Sheep provided milk, meat, and wool for the Israelites. This common sheep was found in the Judean desert and is about to be auctioned at a sheep market in Jerusalem.

Scripture mentions some species of birds that are unfamiliar to us. Some of these are native to the Near East, others are common to many parts of the world (though they are designated in the Bible by less familiar names).

1. Bitterns. The bittern (Hebrew, *kippod*) is a solitary bird whose booming cry echoes mysteriously through the stillness of marshes. Prophets such as Zephaniah felt that the bittern epitomized utter solitude and desolation. The bittern is mentioned three times in Scripture (Isa. 14:23; 34:11; Zeph. 2:14). Isaiah 14:23 probably refers to a long-necked, long-legged wading bird similar to the heron. The other two passages refer to the "short-eared owl."

2. Cormorants. This bird (Hebrew, *kaath* or *shalak*) is linked with the bittern by two biblical writers—Isaiah and Zephaniah—who evidently see them as similar. However, the cormorant is essentially a seabird that lives by catching fish. Perhaps the similarity between the two lies in their solitary and lonely life.

An unclean bird by Levitical law, the cormorant is mentioned four times in the Bible (Lev. 11:17; Deut. 14:17; Isa. 34:11; Zeph. 2:14). The *shalak* is probably the common cormorant or the pygmy cormorant, which breeds at the area formerly occupied by Hula Lake. The Hebrew *kacta* is probably more properly rendered *pelican*. (See below.)

3. Cranes. The crane (Hebrew, *agur*) is one of the largest birds in the Holy Land, with an extended wing span of 2.1 m. (7 ft.) and a standing height of approximately 1.2 m. (4 ft.). The crane has a loud trumpeting voice that resounds as it takes flight. It is a wading bird that feeds on frogs, fish worms, and insects; therefore the

Jews considered it to be unclean. This bird is mentioned twice in Scripture (Isa. 38:14; Jer. 8:7).

4. Cuckoos (Cuckows). Many scholars feel the Hebrew word *shahaph* has been improperly translated as *cuckoo* or *cuckow*. The Bible writers were probably describing some form of sea gull or the common tern. It is unlikely that the two species of cuckoos that do visit Palestine in the summer—the common cuckoo and the great spotted cuckoo—are meant, for they are not flesh-eating birds. The cuckow was considered an unclean bird, so it is mentioned only twice in Scripture (Lev. 11:16; Deut. 14:15).

5. Doves or Turtledoves. Doves were listed as clean birds, and therefore could be eaten and sacrificed. They lived in the craggy holes of rocks and were known for their passive dispositions, never retaliating or resisting their enemies. For this reason, the dove became known as the symbol of peace. Jesus exhorted His followers to be "harmless as doves" (Matt. 10:16), emphasizing the peaceable characteristics that are pleasing to Him. The dove is also a symbol of the Holy Spirit (Luke 3:22).

Four species of doves are found in Palestine: the ringdove or wood pigeon, the stock dove, the rock dove, and the ash-rumped dove.

The Hebrew *yonah* and Greek *peristera* are both rendered as *dove*. This bird is mentioned many times in Scripture (e.g., Gen. 8:8-12; Psa. 55:6; Isa. 38:14; Matt. 3:16; Mark 1:10).

The turtledove (Hebrew, *tor*) is a special type of pigeon. The most abundant in Palestine is the common turtledove. Also found there are the collared turtledove and the palm turtledove. Like the dove, this bird is gentle and harmless; hence in appearance it was an emblem of a defenseless and innocent people (Psa. 74:19). The Israelites often used turtledoves as burnt offerings (Lev. 1:14).

6. Eagles. Bible scholars disagree about which species of eagle is meant by the Hebrew word *resher*. Some think it might be the griffon or great vulture, a bird that is very common in Palestine and adjacent countries. Others believe it may be the golden eagle, which is common in Syria, or the imperial eagle. In any case, the eagle was a bird of high honor in the Bible and was often used as a prophetic symbol.

The eagle displays great tenderness toward its young, but has destructive power as well. It is noted for its ability to fly quickly to high altitudes (Prov. 23:5; Isa. 40:31; Obad. 4). It builds its nest high on cliffs and rocks away from danger. It has long been believed that an eagle renews its strength after molting and takes on the appearance of a young bird (cf. Psa. 103:5).

Small living creatures are the natural food of the eagle; but mainly the bird is a scavenger, feeding on dead carcasses. Though an unclean bird by Levitical law (Lev. 11:13), the eagle is mentioned often in the Bible. Prophets saw the symbol of the eagle in their visions of God (Ezek. 1:10; 10:14; Rev. 4:7).

7. Gier Eagles. This unclean bird (Hebrew, *rahamah*) was the Egyptian vulture. It displays many of the same characteristics as the eagle, and is mentioned twice in the Scriptures (Lev. 11:18; Deut. 14:17).

8. Hawks. Even though God's law designated hawks as unclean, Greeks and Egyptians considered them to be sacred. The Egyptian sun god Re was represented with the head of the hawk.

The hawk (Hebrew, *nea*) is a general name for more than one species of predatory birds known for their fierceness—such as the sparrow hawk and the kestrel. In Scripture, the hawk is mentioned three times (Lev. 11:16; Deut. 14:15; Job 39:26).

9. Herons. Considered unclean because it eats fish, the heron (Hebrew, *anaphah*) is a water fowl. The buff-backed heron is the most common and is often called the white ibis. With it are found the common heron and the purple heron.

10. Kites. This bird (Hebrew, *ayyak*) is said to have extremely keen eyesight. It is an unclean bird of the falcon family and breeds in northern Palestine. In winter, the kite travels extensively.

Various kinds of kites are common to Palestine: the black kite, the yellow-billed kite, and the red kite. The kite is mentioned twice in Scripture (Lev. 11:14; Deut. 14:13).

11. Lapwings. Sometimes called a "hoopoe," the lapwing is a small, double-crested bird of many colors. It is commonly found in Palestine and the warmer parts of the Old World. A lapwing (Hebrew, *dukiphath*) builds its nest in holes along pathways, where travelers pack the earth firmly and prevent invasion by jackals. The lapwing is mentioned twice in Scripture (Lev. 11:19; Deut. 14:18).

12. Nighthawks. Because of its dietary habits, this bird was considered unclean by Levitical law. Some biblical scholars believe the bird (Hebrew, *talmas*) was a barn owl. Others believe it was indeed the familiar nighthawk that abounds in the Near East. While rare in North America, this species thrives in the woodlands of Asia Minor, darting about with the swiftness of a swallow. It is mentioned twice in the Scriptures (Lev. 11:16; Deut. 14:15).

13. Ospreys (Oprays). This bird (Hebrew, *ozniyyah*) feeds on fish and can be found in the vicinity of seas, lakes, rivers, and pools. The Levitical law declared it unclean. Different species of the osprey are found in Europe, Asia, Africa, North America, and Australia. However, the Hebrew word may also refer to the short-toed eagle, the most abundant member of the eagle family in Palestine. It is mentioned twice in Scripture (Lev. 11:13; Deut. 14:12).

14. Ossifrages. Declared an unclean animal by Levitical law, this bird (Hebrew, *peres*) is the bearded vulture or eagle. It was one of the most formidable birds of its tribe; in fact, the name *ossifrage* literally means "bonebreaker." The bird is thus named for its habit of dropping dead animals from great heights onto rocks to crack their bones, in order to eat the bone marrow. The ossifrage lacks

Deer. This ancient Hittite relief shows a hunter pursuing a deer. The Hebrews admired the deer for its grace and speed. It was a clean animal according to the Scriptures (Deut. 14:5), and could be used for food.

the strength of many eagles, so it can't carry off living prey. But its throat muscles give it an enormous swallowing ability. It is mentioned twice in Scripture (Lev. 11:13; Deut. 14:12).

15. Ostriches. The ostrich (Hebrew, *yaen* or *yaanah*) was considered unclean because of its fleshy diet. Ostriches lay eggs in conspicuous places and quickly abandon their eggs or young when danger approaches. An ostrich can easily outrun a horse, though because of its tremendous weight—33 to 36 kg. (70 to 80 lb.)—it cannot fly. Scripture explicitly mentions the ostrich twice (Lam. 4:3; Job 39:13), and other verses may allude to the bird (Isa. 13:21; Mic. 1:8).

16. Owls. Even though it was an unclean bird, the owl is referred to as being "beautiful." It is sometimes referred to as the "mourning owl," because it habitually visits cemeteries.

The owl prefers solitary and desolate surroundings. Combined with its doleful hooting in search of food at night, these characteristics give the owl a dismal reputation. It is common in Egypt and Syria.

The King James Version translates several Hebrew words as "owl"; they may actually refer to different kinds of fowl.

Bath hayyaanah (Lev. 11:16) is probably the ostrich.

Kos (Lev. 11:17; Deut. 14:16; Psa. 102:6) is probably the little owl found throughout Palestine, considered a good-luck omen by Arabs.

Yenshuph or *yanshoph* is the "great owl" (Lev. 11:17; Deut. 14:16), which lives in wastelands (Isa. 34:11). This is probably the Egyptian eagle owl.

Tinshe-meth. See "Swan."

Lilith may have been the screech owl. But some scholars think *lilith* does not refer to an owl (cf. Isa. 34:14).

Kippoz (Isa. 34:15) may be the scops owl, common around ruins in the Near East.

17. Partridges. This bird (Hebrew, *kore*) is very common in Palestine, making its home in mountainous cliffs. The partridge lays its eggs on the sand and rocks, thus exposing them to breakage. Partridge eggs were greatly prized by the ancient Syrians, who gathered them in large numbers. Because of its unwillingness to take flight, the bird was chased on foot until it became exhausted; then the pursuer hit it with a stick or rock. The partridge is mentioned in Jeremiah 17:11.

Two species of partridge are found in Palestine—the desert of Hey's sand partridge and the chukar partridge. The former is the only species of En-gedi, where David compared himself to a hunted partridge (1 Sam. 26:20).

18. Peacocks. It seems from 1 Kings 10:22 and 2 Chronicles 9:21 that King Solomon brought the peacock by ships from abroad. The magnificent bird (Hebrew, *tukkiyyim*) is known by its long tail that trails gracefully behind it. But scholars disagree as to whether the peacock is really the bird that the Scripture writers intended to portray.

In Job 39:13, the "peacock" referred to (Hebrew, *renanim*) is said to have "goodly wings," but there is no mention of the striking tail feathers. It has generally been thought that this text refers to the Indian peacock.

Others feel that the Hebrew word *tukkiyyim* refers to a kind of monkey. The Egyptian word *tkyw* means monkey; this is very similar to *tukkiyyim* without the vowels.

19. Pelicans. The pelican makes its home among the reeds and rushes of lakes and rivers in Western Asia. Toward the end of each day, the pelicans gather in flocks and soar in circles before landing on an island or open plain. When pelicans roost, they form a circle, keeping their heads forward to ward off enemies. The female of the species has a large pouch that can hold up to 11.4 liters (3 gal.) of water and enough food to feed six men. She feeds herself and her young from this pouch. This bird also gorges itself on fish, then flies into the wilderness to sit in some lonely, isolated spot for days, its bill resting on its breast. For this reason, the pelican is used to describe melancholy (Psa. 102:6).

There are two species of pelicans in the Near East—the white pelican and the Dalmatian pelican. Jewish law declared the pelican unclean (Lev. 11:8; Deut. 14:17).

20. Pigeons. This bird was acceptable as an Israelite sacrifice if a person were unable to bring a lamb. In Scripture, the pigeon may be any member of a widely distributed sub-family of birds (*columbinae*). The term *dove* is loosely applied to many of the smaller species found in this sub-family. (See "Dove.") The term "young pigeon" is usually used when referring to its cultic or sacrificial use. The pigeon is almost always mentioned with the turtledove; doves are actually pigeons.

21. Quail. The Lord used quail (Hebrew, *selaw*) to supply food to the Israelites in the wilderness. God caused a mighty wind to bring enough quail to feed them for more than a month (Exod. 16:13). The Israelites spread the quail around the camp to dry in the sun and air (Num. 11:32).

Quail are considered a small game bird of great delicacy. They fly in large flocks across the Mediterranean, sometimes in such numbers as to cover small islands. The quail is weak of wing and often flies with the wind. When it does land, it is often exhausted and easily caught by hand, which is how the Israelites caught them. The quail of Scripture was the European, not American, quail.

22. Ravens. Eight or more species of ravens are found in Palestine. The raven (Hebrew, *oreb*; Greek, *korax*) resembles the crow in size, shape, and color; but its black feathers are more iridescent. Ravens live in pairs and are devoted parents, while crows are so solitary that they drive their young from the nest as soon as they can fend for themselves.

The raven of the Scriptures is undoubtedly the common raven, which is found in all parts of Palestine.

The raven was an unclean bird by the Hebrew law. The world

Hare. Plentiful in Palestine, hares look like large rabbits; but unlike rabbits, they are born with a coat of hair and are able to see at birth. They were considered unclean and forbidden as food to the Israelites (Lev. 11:6).

has commonly portrayed the bird as an omen of evil, but the Bible makes no such connection. In fact, the raven seemed to be favored by God, since it was used to bring meat and bread to the prophet Elijah (1 Kings 17:4, 6). Also, Christ used the raven in His illustration of God's providence (Luke 12:24). Scripture refers to the raven 11 times (e.g., Gen. 8:7; Job 38:41; Psa. 147:9; Prov. 30:17; Isa. 34:11).

23. Sparrows. The Hebrew word *sippor*—rendered *sparrow* in Psalms 84:3 and 102:7—more properly refers to the whole family of small birds that do not feed exclusively on grain. The very poor used sparrows as offerings (Matt. 10:29; Luke 12:6). The sparrow was considered a domestic bird.

24. Storks. An unclean bird by Levitical law (Lev. 11:19; Deut. 14:18), the stork is much like the crane but larger. It feeds on insects, snails, and frogs. The common stork stands about 1.2 m. (4 ft.) high with a wing span of 2.1 m. (7 ft.). The white stork has black only on the tips of its wings. The black stork, also found in Palestine, has a black neck and back. Because of its long legs, the stork can find its food in the water as well as on the land. The bird builds its nest in high places, usually trees or lofty ruins (Psa. 104:17).

In most places where the stork lives, it is protected by man. Ancient people believed that the offspring could recognize its parents throughout its life. The Hebrew word for stork, *hasidah*, meant "affectionate." Storks have powerful wings, and they regularly migrate to Africa. The bird has no vocal organs; the only sound it makes is created by rapidly snapping its long bill, making a sound similar to castanets. The stork is also mentioned in Jeremiah 8:7 and Zechariah 5:9.

25. Swallows. Swallows (Hebrew, *deroi, sus* or *sis*, and *egur*) inhabit the Holy Land in abundance, making their nests atop high places. These migratory birds are known for their swiftness (Prov. 26:2). Some believe that the swift (*cypselus apus*) is meant by these Hebrew words.

26. Swans. The swan (Hebrew, *tinshemeth*) was an unclean bird of great strength, but which rarely attacked any living thing. It is mentioned only twice in Scripture (Lev. 11:18; Deut. 14:16). Some scholars believe that the word actually denotes the white owl. The Old Testament also used *tinshemeth* to refer to a reptile classed with the lizard.

Horus. Egyptians believed the predatory hawk represented the god Horus. This statue of Horus, which dates from the seventh century B.C., wears the crown of Upper and Lower Egypt.

27. Vultures. Different translations apply the Hebrew words for kite, gier eagle, and ossifrage to the vulture. This large bird is a scavenger of flesh, and was therefore considered unclean by Levitical law (Lev. 11:14; Deut. 14:13). Vultures have poor eyesight (Job 28:7) and rely on their sense of smell to locate food. Vultures are also mentioned in Isaiah 34:15.

B. Fish. The subject of fish and fishing weaves its way through much of the Bible. At least seven of the apostles—Peter, Thomas, Nathaniel (probably Bartholomew), John, James the elder, and two additional disciples—made fishing their livelihood upon the Sea of Galilee, or Gennesaret (Matt. 4:18; Luke 5:6-9; John 21:3). We learn in John 21:1-6 that these apostles returned to fishing after Jesus' resurrection. Like many other fishermen of their day, the disciples fished with nets and hooks. They may have also fished with a baited hook at the end of a line. Peter probably fished with pole and hook when Jesus told him to cast a hook and catch a fish for the tribute tax (Matt. 17:27).

The fish quickly became Christianity's chief symbol. Early Christians who gathered for secret meetings in the catacombs of

Rome used the sign of a fish to signal fellow Christians that a meeting was near. They probably chose the Greek word for fish (*ichthus*) as a code for the name of Christ: *Iesous Christos Theou Huios Soter* (Jesus Christ, God's Son, Savior). The first letters of these Greek words combine to make the word *ichthus* in Greek.

1. Species of Fish. The ancient Hebrews caught and ate fish from the many lakes and rivers of Palestine and Syria. Unfortunately, the Bible names no particular kinds of fish that the Hebrews favored. So we must assume they went after the same types of fish that are popular in the Near East today.

a. Freshwater Fish. Fish are plentiful today in the Jordan River and its tributaries, as well as in the other tributaries to the Dead Sea. Even small ponds and fountains in this area have plenty of fish. The pond called Mezereib, near Jordan, and the fountains of Capernaum and Elisha, near Jericho, are well supplied with water life.

The barbel, the bigger species of carp, has grown to such size in the Euphrates River that it is called the "camel fish." The Hebrews probably saw many fish of the "black fish" family. Many scholars believe that the Hebrews generally refused to eat the black fish; but it was held in high esteem by the Romans. Black fish are caught today with a large hook fixed to a pole; this method may be suggested in Matthew 17:27. The catfish may reach large sizes. Josephus recorded that these were present in the Nile.

Carp are still plentiful throughout Syria, where they originated before passing into Europe. The carp was the sacred fish at Urfah, and is found in many other fishponds throughout the Jordan area.

The mormyrus swims upriver, like the bass, and is considered one of the tastiest fish produced in freshwaters. We also find perch, loach, bream, and the common eel in Palestine. Trout are plentiful in its mountain streams, and a species of salmon is among the edible fish of the Nile and the large rivers of Syria.

b. Saltwater Fish. Fish of many different species are still found along Syria's seacoast—barracuda, great sea bream, mackerel, flying fish, gudgeon, mullet, herrings, shad, and sharks and one species of sea mammal.

We are told that "God created great whales" (Gen. 1:21). By the term *whale,* the ancients no doubt meant sea monsters in general. The root of the Hebrew word for whale (*tan*) clearly suggests a creature of great length—without necessarily meaning that the creature was a sea animal. In fact, *tan* is often translated *dragon* or *leviathan*, but *dragon* is incorrect. From other Semitic languages such as Ugaritic we know that both *tanin* and *leviathan* refer to whales.

Neither the Old nor the New Testament clearly states that a whale swallowed Jonah, although the King James Version improperly uses this term in Matthew 12:40. Scripture tells us simply that Jonah was swallowed by a "great fish" (Jon. 1:17).

But whales were not unknown in the Mediterranean. Sightings of whales have been recorded in this area occasionally throughout history. The whales most likely to be encountered would be the humpback whale and the fin whale.

Toothed whales were probably more common in early times than at present. In fact, the bones of a great toothed whale were on exhibit in pre-Roman times at a pagan temple at Joppa (now called Jaffa), the very place from which Jonah set sail. At the time, legend said these were the bones of a dragon monster slain by Perseus. The bones remained at Joppa until conquering Romans carried them triumphantly home to their capital.

2. Methods of Fishing. We can see people in the act of fishing in Egyptian and Assyrian sculptures and paintings. These show us that the ancients used methods of fishing very similar to those used by fishermen today. They employed the line and hook, rod and hook, rod and line, and net.

a. Nets. The ancient Hebrews used nets for fishing and hunting. Scripture mentions several kinds of nets for different purposes. The Hebrew word *cherem* denoted a net used for either fishing or hunting (Ezek. 26:5, 14; 47:10; Hab. 1:15, 17). The word *mikmōreth* denoted the net of a fisherman (Isa. 19:8; cf. Hab. 1:15-16, where "drag" is a rendering of the same word).

The New Testament mentions the use of nets for fishing only. We believe the ancient Hebrews used woven nets much like the nets of Egypt, which are mentioned more than once in Scripture (cf. Isa. 19:8).

b. Hooks and Rods. The Egyptians mastered the art of catching fish by hook in ancient times. Job 41:1-7 suggests that very large fish were probably caught with hooks or spears. The apostles who fished upon the Sea of Galilee probably used hooks and rods, as well as nets (Matt. 17:27).

3. Fish in Ancient Trade. Laws concerning fish as food (Lev. 11:9-12; Deut. 14:9-10) suggest that the methods of catching fish were known even in the time of the Exodus. Fishermen may have used the net even in Egypt's early period (Job 18:8; 19:6). They preserved fish in pools, from which the prey was easily taken (Song of Sol. 7:4; Isa. 19:10).

Mosaic law declared that fish having scales and fins were proper for food, while those without scales were unclean (Lev. 11:9-10). This ruled out eels, sharks, and some other saltwater creatures. The Jews in the wilderness fondly remember the fish that they ate in Egypt (Num. 11:5), but we do not know which kinds of fish they recalled. Fish was a favorite food in the Promised Land so we assume that the Israelites found a ready supply in the lakes and rivers from Palestine and Syria, as well as in the sea.

Freshwater fish, especially the black fish, were salted like sea fish. The historian Strabo (808-849) tells us that the fish wharf of

---

What Swallowed Jonah?

As long as there are little children, Bible storybooks, and Sunday schools, the story of Jonah will be told. Some of those storybooks will tell about Jonah and the whale, and some will tell about Jonah and the great fish. Which is right?

The answer seems simple enough if one checks only the Book of Jonah. Virtually every English translation says that Jonah was swallowed by a "great fish" (Jon. 1:17). Other verses (2:1, 10) refer only to "the fish."

Yet when Jesus refers to the story of Jonah in Matthew 12:40, He says, "For as Jonah was three days and three nights in the whale's belly; so shall the Son of man be three days and three nights in the heart of the earth." Thus the confusion.

Jonah began his voyage at the seaport of Joppa, which is on the Mediterranean Sea. Very few whales are found in the Mediterranean. But the sperm whale, which is sometimes found here, can swallow a person whole.

A 30-m. (100-ft.) whale captured off Cape Cod in 1933 had a mouth nearly 4 m. (12 ft.) wide. This was easily large enough to have engulfed a man. Interestingly, an enlargement of the whale's nasal sinus provided a storage compartment of air.

A newspaper article in the *Cleveland* (Ohio) *Plain Dealer* reported that Dr. Ransome Harvey found a little dog in the head of a whale after it had fallen from a ship 6 days earlier. Dr. Harry Rimmer, President of the Research Science Bureau of Los Angeles, has documented reports from the 1920s which tell of a sailor being rescued from the stomach of a shark 48 hours after he had been swallowed.

What swallowed Jonah? We can't be certain. But whatever it was, it caused him to repent of his stubbornness and carry God's message to Nineveh.

Taricheaea on the Sea of Galilee got its name from this practice.

The Jews enjoyed eating and trading sea fish quite as much as fresh fish. Sidon got its name from being a popular place where fish trade was carried on. We learn from Nehemiah 13:16 that the Phoenicians of Tyre frequented Jerusalem as fish dealers.

A gate on Jerusalem's northeast border was named the Fish Gate (2 Chron. 33:14; Neh. 3:3; 12:39; Zeph. 1:10). This gate is elsewhere called "the first gate" (Zech. 14:10). Some Bible scholars believe that fish from the Sea of Galilee were brought in through this gate.

REPTILES AND INSECTS

It seems as though most of the animals mentioned in the Bible are big, colorful ones that do spectacular things. But notice how many history-making events in the Bible turn on the actions of small reptiles and insects.

Sin and temptation were first introduced by the actions of a snake (cf. Gen. 3). Three of the terrible plagues that God sent upon the Egyptians were plagues of insects—lice, flies, and locusts (Exod. 8:16-32; 10:1-20). Aaron proved that God was with him by turning his rod into a snake (Exod. 7:8-12). John the Baptist lived on locusts and wild honey made by bees (Mark 1:6). In fact, the Promised Land was described as a land "that floweth with milk and honey" (Lev. 20:24).

A *reptile* is an animal, always cold-blooded, that zoologists classify between birds and amphibians in its complexity of physical structure. The reptiles of the Bible are much like the ones we know: snakes, lizards, turtles, crocodiles, and so on.

Likewise, insects of biblical times were very much like the ones we know. Flies, grasshoppers, beetles, and mosquitoes are commonly known insects. Many different insects are mentioned in the Bible.

A. Why They Flourished. Several factors combined to give reptiles and insects a notable influence upon the lives of the Hebrew people.

1. Climate. The climate of the Holy Land varied greatly for such a small nation. High mountains, dry deserts, hot river valleys and barren, stony ground gave opportunity for a wide variety of insects and reptiles to make their homes in the land. In the desert, lizards abounded and the sand fleas made life miserable for the wandering Hebrew people. Flies also swarmed in hot, jungle-like lowlands and in the desert in summer.

2. Inadequate Control. Man had little control over nature in Bible times; there were no insecticides and no insight into the diseases that some insects carried. The semi-nomadic life of the early Hebrews brought them into contact with a wide variety of reptiles and insects, and their lack of knowledge about these creatures often brought hardships.

3. Food Value. Unlike our Western culture today, many Near Eastern societies used reptiles and insects for food. Reptiles were considered unclean among the Israelites, but neighboring people did eat snakes, lizards, and turtles. Even the Hebrews were permitted to eat locusts, grasshoppers, and perhaps beetles (Lev. 12:22).

In taking a look at the reptiles and insects of the Bible, we need to remember the Bible is an ancient Semitic book, so many of the terms it uses are inexact by our standards. (For example, we really don't know what organism is meant in many places where the word *lice* is used.) Even so, the Bible gives us some interesting glimpses of the reptiles and insects that were familiar to the Israelites and early Christians of Palestine. (These species are still there today.)

B. Reptiles. Reptiles were the earliest living things; in fact, they were created on the same day as man (cf. Gen. 1:24-25, where "creeping thing" is usually interpreted to mean reptiles and insects).

1. Chameleons. *Chameleon* is the King James Version's rendering of two Hebrew words, *tinshemeth* and *koah*. The chameleon is listed as an unclean animal (Lev. 11:30).

2. Lizards. Called *leta'ah* in Hebrew, lizards were regarded as unclean (Lev. 11:30).

In Bible lands, green lizards were plentiful in cultivated land and in woods. Much of the present land of Israel was covered with thick forests in Bible times; agriculture has stripped much of this wooded land.

Wall lizards of the same *Lacertidue* family also abounded in farm

Ostrich. Ostriches once inhabited the semi-desert areas of Israel. Considered unclean and "cruel" by the early Israelites (Lam. 4:3), the ostrich lays its eggs in conspicuous places and quickly deserts them when danger approaches. The birds are too heavy to fly, but can easily outrun a horse.

areas, crawling over any stony surface available. The warm weather associated with the growing season brought out many varieties of lizards.

The yellowish lizards of the dry desert lands hid under rocks and burrowed in the ground, but didn't climb well. The sandy deserts often produced lizards up to 61 cm. (2 ft.) in length.

Southern Judea had "land monitors" that were from 1 to 1.5 m. (4 to 5 ft.) in length and lived as far south as the Sinai. They had long snouts with sharp, pointed teeth and long tails. Leviticus 11:30 refers to this type of lizard. "Water monitors" lived in the streams, rivers and lakes of the area. They were even larger and could be quickly identified in the water by the high ridge of their backs.

3. **Snakes (Serpents).** The word *serpent* is used in the Bible as freely as we now use the word *snake*. In Genesis 49:17, *adder* (Hebrew, *shephiphon*) probably refers to the horned sand snake of Arabia and Egypt. This poisonous snake often coils and waits—perhaps in a sandy imprint of a camel's hoof—until a small animal comes along. Then it strikes, bites, poisons its victim, and kills for food. Most mature animals can smell the adder and are terribly afraid of it.

The Hebrew word *pethen* in Psalms 58:4 and 91:13 probably refers to the Egyptian cobra, *Naja hāje*. Some feel that another Hebrew word for adder (*aksub*, as in Psa. 140:3; Prov. 23:32) might mean the horn viper, the puff adder, or the common adder. The Septuagint translators believed this word in Psalm 5:9 referred to the asp; so did Paul when he quoted this verse in Romans 3:13.

The "asp" (Hebrew, *pethen*) is also thought to refer to the Egyptian cobra (see above), for it was said to live in holes in the ground. The asp was small and very poisonous (Deut. 32:33), for it was most dangerous to allow an infant child to play at the hole of such a snake (Isa. 11:8).

The Egyptian cobra has a hood that flares when it is about to strike. Its diet consists of frogs and mice. It has been called "the spitter," due to its habit of spitting just before it bites. Queen Cleopatra of Egypt is said to have committed suicide by putting an asp to her breast.

The King James Version of the Bible uses the word *cockatrice* for a very poisonous snake (Isa. 11:8; 14:29; Jer. 8:17), although we cannot identify exactly what snake is meant by the Hebrew phrase behind it. Some think it is the yellow viper, some the cerastes, and others think the King James Version uses the term to apply to any venomous serpent. The Hebrew terms *siph'oni* and *seph'a* are rendered *cockatrice* in some passages but *adder* in others.

Viper is the King James Version's rendering of the Hebrew word *'eph'eh*. The Old Testament use of this word is unclear and could mean any of several snakes (cf. Job 20:16; Isa. 30:6).

The most familiar New Testament reference to a viper is in Acts 28:1-6, which tells how Paul was bitten by one. But the New Testament word (*echidna*) can also be used for any poisonous snake. The passage in Acts 28 probably refers to the common viper, which is often found on the Mediterranean coast. Vipers were different from other snakes in that they gave live birth to their young, instead of laying eggs.

The "brass serpent" of Numbers 21 indicates a classical respect for snakes; they are still highly regarded in some places today. At God's command, Moses erected a brass snake on a pole so that people who had been bitten by live snakes could look at it and be healed. The New Testament's direct symbolism of the "brass serpent" (cf. John 3:14-15) refers to Jesus' death on the cross. The serpent has become an important symbol in other instances too.

4. Other Reptiles. One whole section of reptile study in the Bible could concern itself with what appears to have been a giant land/water animal. It has been variously translated as *dragon, whale,* and *satyr* in the Old Testament; the only New Testament reference to this creature (Rev. 12:3-17ff.) is translated simply as *dragon.*

Most likely these animals were crocodiles (cf. Psa. 74:13; Isa. 34:14; Jer. 51:34). Whales are also a possibility, but the Bible writers were more familiar with whales and probably would have identified them as such. Most New Testament scholars agree that the use of *dragon* in the Book of Revelation is a symbolic reference to Satan and not to an actual dragon.

Again, the *leviathan* (Hebrew, *livyathan*) in Job 41 probably refers to the Nile crocodile. In two other places similar reference is made (Psa. 74:14; Isa. 27:1). However, in Psalm 104:26 *livyathan* probably means a whale.

There were indeed many crocodiles in Bible lands in former centuries. However, man's taming of the land has crowded out the mighty crocodile; the last one was killed in the Jordan River in the mid-1800s, and there have not been any since.

INSECTS

For every star you can see in the sky on a clear night, scientists have estimated that there are 100 kinds of insects—a total of over 800,000 kinds. There are billions of insects of each kind. Throughout history, insects have covered the earth in great numbers.

Some insects are mentioned in the Bible as they affected events and people. Others are mentioned to illustrate a spiritual truth. Locusts and other locust-like insects are the most often mentioned, but others are frequently more important.

Of one thing we may be sure: In the Mediterranean area with its

Fishing Boats.
Fishermen cast their nets while moored at the Sea of Galilee, north of Tiberias. Snow-topped Mount Hermon rises majestically above the northern shores of the lake, which has provided food for the region from antiquity.

heat, humidity, and poor health conditions, insects were a sad fact of everyday life for the Israelites.

A. Ants. Two sections of the Book of Proverbs mention ants in order to point out the hard-working nature of these tiny insects. Proverbs 6:6-8 and 30:25 point out that ants work without supervision and plan ahead for times when food will be scarce.

Ants are any of the myriad insects belonging to the *Formicidae* family. There are 104 types of ants in the Eastern Hemisphere and only two are "harvesting ants," as described in Proverbs. These ants nested near grain fields, threshing floors, or granaries. Since the harvester ants also collected their grain from the sown seed, they often prevented germination entirely.

The people in Bible Lands accepted and even admired the ants for their hard work. Historical records outside the Bible document the presence of ants from earliest times.

B. Bees and Hornets. Bees and wasps (called "hornet wasps" in the Hebrew, from a word that refers to their stinging power) are "social insects" that cooperate to do their work. The honeybee seems to be the only variety in the Bible, for each time that Scripture describes the bee, it also mentions the fact that it produces honey.

Samson found a swarm of bees in a lion carcass (Judg. 14:8), and wild bees placed honey in other odd locations (Deut. 32:13; Psa. 81:16).

The Septuagint rendering of Proverbs 6:8 tells us, "Go to the bee, and learn how diligent she is, and how earnestly she is engaged in her work, whose labours kings and private men use for health, and she is desired and respected by all. Though weak in body she is advanced by honouring wisdom." Obviously the ancient writers admired the bee's industrious traits.

Honey was the most highly prized sweet treat of the Bible (1 Kings 14:3; Song of Sol. 5:1; Ezek. 27:17). This was another reason for this insect's good reputation.

While the bee produced something that man desired, the hornet or wasp was a pest. The Hebrew word for hornet is *sir'ah*. This insect is of the same genus as the wasp, but it is larger and more vicious. The hornet's troubles for man are described in Exodus 23:28, Deuteronomy 7:20, and Joshua 24:12. These small, stinging flyers could do much harm; ancient secular accounts tell of whole cities that had to flee from swarms of wasps or hornets.

As the Bible records, God used these tiny fighters to teach His

Fish. Fish from the Sea of Galilee are as important to the diet of the modern Israelis as they were to their ancestors. In 1965, the Sea of Galilee yielded 304 tons of this particular species, the Tilapia.

people much-needed lessons. Read, for example, Deuteronomy 7:20-23.

C. Beetles, Crickets. Biblical references to "beetles" or "crickets" (Lev. 11:22) seem to be a poor translation of the Hebrew word *hargāl*. The Hebrew word most likely refers to one of the three related families of insects—locusts, grasshoppers, or crickets. However, there can be little doubt that many varieties of true beetles did live in the Bible lands, among them the house cricket and the field cricket. Some experts feel that Exodus 8:21 refers to a true beetle, since the Egyptians worshiped the beetle as a god of fertility and immortality.

D. Caterpillars. The caterpillar (also the *cankerworm* of Joel 1:4; Nah. 3:15-16, and the *palmerworm* of Joel 1:4) was a wormlike crawler that may simply have been an earlier developmental stage of the locust.

The caterpillar (Hebrew, *hasil*) devoured foodstuffs, according to the Bible (1 Kings 8:37). Thus God sometimes used the caterpillar as a punishment (Psa. 78:46; 105:34).

The cankerworm (Hebrew, *yelek*) may also have been the locust in one of its molting stages. In this stage, the insect is even more to be dreaded than as a mature creature.

The palmerworm (Hebrew, *gayam*—the word means "pilgrim worm") mentioned in Joel 1:4 is known for its wide-ranging habits. One translation calls it "creeping locust," as though it were the same insect as the locust, without wings. Its destructiveness is well described in Amos 4:9.

E. Fleas. Fleas (Hebrew, *par'osh*) live on the blood of animals and make their homes on and under the skin of animals. The flea's ability to leap is astounding; it can jump 200 times its own body length.

Fleas were well-known pests in Bible times, but the insect is mentioned only twice in Scripture (1 Sam. 24:14; 26:20). The area around Tiberias was known for having many terrible fleas. A popular saying was that the king of the fleas had his court in Tiberias.

F. Flies. Flies have been pests to man since the beginning of time. But in our English Bibles, the word *fly* refers to any one of a variety of bothersome insects. The plague of flies (Hebrew, *arab*) in Exodus 8:21ff. probably refers to a mixture of tiny insects. It could mean that flies, mosquitoes, and many other kinds of bugs plagued the Egyptians. (*See* "Beetles, Crickets.")

The phrase "diverse sorts of flies" in Psalm 78:45 continues that idea. Yet some translations of the Bible take this phrase to mean "dog fly" or "gadfly."

We who live in more temperate climates cannot comprehend the abundance of flies in the Bible lands. Cattle were literally bothered to death by them. Larger flies so troubled humans with their bites that deaths were credited to them. The heat, the lack of sanitation, and the people's inability to fight the flies only added to their numbers.

Farming has always been difficult in the Holy Land, and the pests such as flies only made the task harder. One tribe—the Ekronites—worshiped a god they called *Baal-zebub* ("the lord of flies"), because they believed he controlled the flies (2 Kings 1:2). The Hebrew word *zebub* meant one of the order *Diptera*, especially the domestic fly.

Cobra or Asp. The desert cobra is a glossy black snake found in Israel and throughout the Middle East. It does not rear up or have a hood like the Egyptian or Indian Cobra. Some think Ecclesiastes 10:11 refers to this snake.

In Ecclesiastes 10:1, the writer likens a little folly to the trouble caused by a few flies (again the Hebrew, *zebub*). The flies laid eggs under the skin of some animals, which brought painful ulcers.

G. Gnats. These tiny pests are in the same family as the mosquito and are an extremely troublesome insect. They grow and reproduce in wet climates and move about mainly at night. The only time the gnat is mentioned in the Bible is in reference to its small size (Matt. 23:24).

H. Lice. Lice (or ticks) are mentioned as the third plague on Egypt in Exodus 8:16. Lice are parasitic pests that live on the skin of animals and humans. Perhaps the sand fly is meant in Exodus 8:16, since "dust" is mentioned in this passage. Both sand flies and lice are common in the Nile Valley. Two Hebrew words (*kinnam* or *kinnim*) are translated both as *lice* and *gnats*.

I. Locusts. Great clouds of locusts have been mentioned in the earliest records of man. They are still seen today, especially in the Near East. The King James Version uses seven different names to refer to the same insect that one Hebrew word (*'arbeh*) records—the locust, bald locust, beetle, cankerworm, caterpillar, grasshopper, and palmerworm.

1. True Locusts. English Bibles often use the word *locust* as the rendering of the Hebrew *'arbeh*. This word probably refers to the migratory locust or similar insects. Migratory locusts are about 5 to 8 cm. (2 to 3 in.) long and move throughout their lives, searching for food. They travel in large swarms and cause a great deal of destruction by their eating habits. These locusts should not be confused with 17-year locust, which North Americans commonly call the "locust."

Migratory locusts eat vegetation of any kind. The huge swarms can strip fields, trees, grasslands, and any other plant life in their path. Their wings carry them upward, where they travel much like gliders; locusts have been known to sail for 160 km. (100 mi.) or more before coming down.

They land at night in trees or in grasses. When the morning sun comes up, they take off again to find food.

When locusts come to a river, they try to fly over. If wind currents do not carry them across, they simply fall into the river by the thousands, forming a bridge for the other locusts. Thus even in

Locusts. Great clouds of locusts still periodically devour crops and forests, especially in the Middle East. The picture at left shows a fig tree in full leaf. The second picture, taken 15 minutes later, shows how a swarm of locusts has stripped the tree bare of all greenery.

dying they cause trouble; downstream the millions of dead locusts become a breeding ground for disease.

Read of the destruction of crops by locusts in Joel 1:1-12. The Romans called them the "burners of the land," because of the destruction they caused.

Farmers have tried many ways of fighting oncoming locusts; the most popular method through the centuries has been to start fires, in hopes that the smoke would steer them away. Even this is not entirely successful.

Mosaic law allowed the Hebrews to eat locusts (Lev. 11:22; Matt 3:4). However, some think that John the Baptist's food was not the locust, but the fruit of the carob tree—"husks" much like the prodigal son ate (Mark 1:6; Luke 15:16). The most popular way to prepare locusts for eating was to dry them, put them in a sack, and simply make them available for visitors to "dig in" and eat as snacks.

Other Bible references to locusts speak of God's judgment and punishment by plagues of locusts (Exod. 10:4-15; Deut. 28:38-42; 1 Kings 8:37; Joel 2:1-11). In Joel 2:25, the invading armies are compared to a swarm of locusts.

2. Grasshoppers. Our English Bibles mention the *grasshopper* in Judges 6:5, Job 39:20, Ecclesiastes 12:5, and Jeremiah 46:23. The destructiveness of grasshoppers is described in Amos 7:1. The Bible also uses the grasshopper as an example of something that has little importance or value (Num. 13:33; Isa. 40:22).

In biblical parlance, the main difference between locusts and grasshoppers lies in the insect's ability to fly. The locusts take wing and go great distances, while the grasshopper "hops" on the ground.

Grasshopper is the English rendering of four Hebrew words: *'arbeh* (as is *locust*), *hagab, gob,* and *gobay*. The second word (found in Lev. 11:22; Num. 13:33; Eccl. 12:5; Isa. 40:22) is probably referring to the English grasshopper.

J. Moths. In the Bible, this word refers to the ordinary genus clothes moth, of which there were several species in Israel. Both the worm stage and the full-grown moth were a threat to clothing in Bible times.

Jesus referred to the moth as a constant threat to man's savings for the future (Matt. 6:19-20). This statement refers to material goods, since there was no paper money in biblical times. The ancients had no mothballs, so it was risky business for them to store clothing and other fragile goods for the future.

Moths are mentioned elsewhere (Job 13:28; Psa. 39:11; Isa. 50:9; Hos. 5:12; James 5:12). Job 4:19 uses the moth as a symbol of vulnerability.

K. Spiders. The Bible symbolically emphasizes the weakness of the spider's web. These tiny insects were known from the beginning of time, and the climate and life-style of Bible times must have made them very common. Indeed, over 600 varieties of spiders have been identified in Palestine.

Job 8:14 and Isaiah 59:5 mention the spider's web as both marvelous and easy to destroy. In the same way, Scripture says that man has false hope if he trusts in his own strength. In these verses, *spider* is a rendering of the Hebrew word *akkabish*.

L. Worms. The insect called *worm* (generally translating the Hebrew *toleah* or *tolath*) might have been any number of other creatures. Perhaps it was the common earthworm or the maggot so familiar in Bible times as the consumer of dead flesh.

When the Bible speaks of man as a worm, it probably means the common earthworm. But other varieties are meant when Exodus 16:24 says there were no "worms" in the manna; and when Deuteronomy 28:39 speaks of "worms" in the vines. Still other worms preyed on human flesh (Job 7:5; Isa. 14:11). Luke writes that Herod Agrippa had a terrible affliction of worms (Acts 12:23).

The "horseleech" mentioned in Proverbs 30:15 was a well-known Palestinian worm that lived in stagnant waters. It fastened itself to the nose or mouth of animals that drank from the water. Once in the animal, it multiplied quickly and lived on the animal's blood, finally killing its host. The Hebrew for *horseleech* was *alukah*.

CLEAN AND UNCLEAN ANIMALS

Even before the Flood, animals fell into these two divisions. Noah was told to take into the ark seven pairs of clean beasts and two pairs of unclean beasts (Gen. 7:2). At that time animals were not eaten, so the clean/unclean designation was probably for sacrifices. When Noah and his family left the ark, God told them,

Could the Ark Hold the Animals?

Children as well as adults find their imaginations stirred by the Old Testament's account of Noah building an enormous ark and gathering the animals, and of the great Flood that covered the earth.

Many have often wondered whether such an ark could really have held so many animals. Encyclopedias tell us that there are about 500,000 species of animals on earth, yet Noah brought the animals into the ark by pairs and sometimes groups of seven. Imagine the space required to contain them and their food supply for a year!

The Bible tells us the ark was 300 cubits long, 50 cubits wide, and 30 cubits high. The cubit was a common unit of measurement in ancient times, but the length of a cubit was determined differently by each nation. Some considered a cubit to be the distance from the elbow to the middle finger; others thought it to be the distance of the entire arm; while still others measured it as the length of a newborn baby. A cubit could vary in length from about 45 to 58 cm. (18 to 22½ in.). Using the cubit's lower standard of 45 cm., we find that the ark measured 22½ by 135 m. (75 by 450 ft.) with a height of 13½ m. (45 ft.). That would make the ark considerably larger than a football field and about three stories high. The ark was divided into three floors, providing a total of 3,037 sq. m. (101,250 sq. ft.) of living area. All this space was usable, since the ark did not require engines to propel it through the water.

Even with such a tremendous capacity, could the ark have housed the animals described in the Bible? To answer that question, we must determine what Genesis means by the term *kind* (Gen. 3:7). Some scholars feel that *kind* approximates our modern classification of "family," which would put the maximum number of animals on the ark at about 700. But other scholars feel that *kind* refers to species instead of animal "families." There are approximately 1,072,300 animal species (a figure provided by the American taxonomist Ernst Mayer), and many did not need to be aboard. Fish, sponges, many insects, and amphibians would have survived the flood waters. But even if we assume that as many as 50,000 animals were on the ark, there was sufficient room to accommodate them.

"Every moving thing that liveth shall be meat for you; even as the green herb have I given you all things" (Gen. 9:3).

Later Moses included dietary restrictions in the Law he handed down to the Israelites. Only certain creatures would be acceptable as food, that is, clean. The Lord told Moses, "Whatsoever parteth the hoof, and is clovenfooted, and cheweth the cud, among the beasts, that shall ye eat" (Lev. 11:3). Basically the clean animals were ruminants, grazing animals which swallow their food quickly and bring it up later in small quantities to chew as a cud. Cattle, sheep and goats, and such wild game as deer and antelope fit this requirement. Yet ruminants without a cloven hoof—the camel for one—were unclean (Lev. 11:4-8).

ANIMALS IN WORSHIP

Though animal sacrifice seems repulsive to modern readers, it was the acceptable method of worship in ancient times. The Israelites at least refrained from human sacrifice, which was all too common among their peers. The first sacrifice the Bible tells of was Abel's. Adam and Eve's second son "brought of the firstlings of his flock and of the fat thereof. And the LORD had respect unto Abel and to his offering" (Gen. 4:4). His brother's offering of "the fruit of the ground" was not accepted.

In a sense, the sacrifice of animals for man's propitiation was a measure of God's mercy. For some crimes no animal substitution was permitted; the sinner's life must be forfeited. When it was possible, the Israelites redeemed their own lives by offering an animal.

Only three kinds of animals were offered in sacrifice, in addition to birds. These were cattle (oxen), sheep, and goats. The kind of animal to be sacrificed depended not on the seriousness of the sin, but on the social standing of the sinner. Thus a priest who sinned had to offer a bullock, a ruler required a male kid, and the common people could get by with only a female kid or a lamb (Lev. 4). Pigeons or turtledoves were an acceptable substitute for people who could not afford even that much. Whatever the animal, it was to be perfect, worthy of sacrifice. (An exception is found in Lev. 22:23).

4

PLANTS AND HERBS
OF PALESTINE

From the beginning of Bible history, the land of Palestine has supplied a sufficient amount of food for the people and their cattle. The people of Bible lands found a use for nearly every plant, from the forests on Mount Lebanon to the scrubby shrubs of the desert.

The three main crops of Palestine were "wine that maketh glad the heart of man, and oil to make his face to shine, and bread [grain] which strengtheneth man's heart" (Psa. 104:15).

GRAINS

Grain has always been one of the main ingredients in man's diet. Various grains have been grown where climate and soil conditions allow. Especially rich were the areas of the Tigris and Euphrates Rivers in the east, the Nile River in Egypt, and the Jordan Valley of Palestine.

Grain was used in many different ways in Bible times: for export, for food, and for sacrificial offerings (Gen. 4:3; Lev. 2:1). Also, Jesus used grain as an object for teaching, as in His parable of the sower (Mark 4:3) and His teaching about the Sabbath (Matt. 12:1).

Grain ("corn") and wine are used in the Old Testament as symbols of plenty and prosperity. In Deuteronomy 11:14, grain is mentioned as a gift of God; in Deuteronomy 18:4, it is described as an offering of obedience; and in Deuteronomy 28:51, the loss of grain is foretold as a warning of Israel's destruction.

When threshing season began, the grains were tossed into the air to remove the chaff. Isaiah suggests that the chaff was later burned (Isa. 5:24).

A. Barley. The Hebrew word for barley is *seorah*, meaning "a hairy or bristling thing." It was so called because of the rough and prickly beard covering the ears. Barley belongs to the genus *Hordeum*, which was cultivated in Palestine (Ruth 1:22), in Egypt (Exod. 9:31), and in adjacent regions.

Barley was used in ceremonial offerings (Num. 5:15), baked into cakes (Judg. 7:13), and fed to horses and camels (1 Kings 4:28). Jesus used barley loaves to feed the five thousand (John 6:9). For food, it was held in low esteem and was believed to be a symbol of poverty. According to Adam Clarke, barley had scarcely one-third the value of wheat in ancient trade.[1]

B. Corn. When Americans or Britons think of corn and cornfields, they visualize long rows of tall, green stalks, tasseling for the harvest. This is not what the Bible means by "corn." In fact, the plant we now call "corn" was introduced to us by the American Indians who called it "maize."

When the King James Version speaks of "corn" in Mark 4:28 and Matthew 12:1, the Bible actually means "grain." The Revised Standard Version correctly uses this term instead of "corn."

C. Millet. The Hebrew word for millet is *dohan*. This term might refer to at least two kinds of grain. One is the cultivated grass known as *Panicum miliaceum*, the other is *Sorghum vulgare*. Both of these grains were cultivated in Palestine, Egypt, and other parts of the ancient world. God instructed Ezekiel to use "millet" for bread (Ezek. 4:9), and it was probably a staple item in the Israelite diet.

D. Rye. The Hebrew word for rye, mentioned in Exodus 9:32, is *kussemeth*, meaning "hairy or bearded grain." The same Hebrew noun is used in Ezekiel 4:9, where the King James Version has *fitches*. The Revised Standard Version translates it as *spelt*.

It is generally believed that this grain had less food value than wheat and was mixed with other grains to make bread (Ezek. 4:9). The Hebrew word may also refer to another inferior grain, emmer, which grows in the area today. Spelt is no longer grown there.

E. Wheat. The Hebrew word for wheat is *hittah*. The kind grown in biblical Egypt (Gen. 41:5-7) is believed to have been the variety with many heads on one stalk. This may also have been the kind of wheat grown in Palestine; but some scholars believe that another species was the "wheat" of Palestine.

Whatever the species, wheat had been cultivated from earliest times in Palestine, Egypt, and Mesopotamia. In Egypt it was grown in abundance and was exported during early Christian times (Acts 27:38).

VEGETABLES

Everywhere the Hebrew people traveled, they included vegetables in their diet. Vegetables were boiled, eaten raw, or mixed with other foods. Some of the vegetables we have today have been known from ancient times.

A. Beans. The "beans" mentioned in the Bible were not found on a bushy plant like the beans of North America or Great Britain, although they were of the same family. The plant grew 91 cm. (3 ft.) high, with white pea-shaped blooms. The beans are large, coarse seeds. Sometimes the Israelites mixed these beans with

Stalks of Wheat. Wheat was cultivated throughout Palestine, Egypt, and Mesopotamia from the earliest times. An important part of the diet of the Israelites (Ruth 2:23), wheat became a symbol of God's goodness and provision (Psa. 81:16).

other grain for bread (2 Sam. 17:28; Ezek. 4:9). Generally, these beans were eaten by the poorer classes of people.

B. Cucumbers. The Hebrew word for cucumber, *kishshu'ah,* could refer to either of two species of cucumbers grown in Egypt and Palestine today.

As Moses led the people through the desert, they still longed for the cucumbers of Egypt (Num. 11:5). Later they planted cucumber gardens in Palestine (Isa. 1:8); in this text, the "lodge in a garden of cucumbers" refers to a shelter used by watchmen to guard the crops.

C. Gourds. The gourd that shaded Jonah (Jon. 4:6-10) may have been either the castor-oil plant or the pumpkin. Either of these could be considered a member of the gourd family.

Most scholars believe that the Hebrew word for gourd (*kikayon*) refers to the castor-oil plant. (This word is similar to the Egyptian word for the castor-oil plant, *kiki.*) The castor-oil plant grows rapidly up to 4.6 m (15 ft.), with purplish-red stems, broad leaves, and fiery red fruit. Any slight injury causes it to wilt. Grown in Southern Asia and Egypt, it is sometimes referred to as the "Christ Palm."

The wild gourd (Hebrew, *pakkuoth*) mentioned in 2 Kings 4:39 was gathered in Gilgal near Jericho and was very poisonous. It was a wild vine of the gourd family that flourished during extreme droughts. The fruit was gourd-like, 8 or more centimeters (3 or more inches) in diameter. Images of the same fruit (called *knops* in 1 Kings 6:18; 7:24) were carved in the cedar beams of Solomon's Temple.

Some botanists believe that the plant *Ecballium elaterium* was the "wild gourd" of 2 Kings 4:39. Although the fruit of this plant was similar to the wild gourd, the plant grew upright with no tendrils, and could hardly have been the vine referred to.

D. Leeks. The Hebrew word *hasir* (spelled *chatzir* in Num. 11:5) usually meant grass. But Numbers 11:5 probably refers to the leek, which grew extensively in Egypt. When the children of Israel grew tired of eating manna, they remembered the foods of Egypt that they considered to be delicacies, such as the leek.

E. Lentils. This plant is from the pea family. The Hebrew word for lentils is *adhashim*. It has five or six pairs of oblong leaves on each stem and white, violet-striped flowers. These legumes are harvested and boiled to produce the red pottage mentioned in Genesis 25:30.

Lentils are grown in all parts of Palestine (cf. 2 Sam. 23:11). They were combined with other ingredients to make bread (Ezek. 4:9).

The *pulse* mentioned in Daniel 1:12, 16 and in 2 Samuel 17:23 is believed to have been the lentil plant.

F. Mandrakes. Mentioned in only two passages in the Bible (Gen. 30:14-16; Song of Sol. 7:13), mandrakes were thought to aid fertility. The Hebrew word for this plant was *dudaim*.

We do not know whether the mandrakes of the Bible were the same as the plant known as the mandrake in Palestine today. This plant has a large forked root with broad, wavy leaves sprouting from the base. The small purple flowers produce yellow fruit. Song of Solomon 7:13 notes the mandrakes' strong fragrance.

G. Onions. The only mention of the onion in the Bible is Numbers 11:5. The Hebrew word is *basal*. Grown in Egypt and other parts of the East, these onions are very large and of exceptional flavor.

HERBS AND SPICES

This large group of plants were in abundant supply in Bible times. They were found growing on mountains, hillsides, along riverbanks, and in valleys. Herbs grew wild in fields and were sometimes cultivated in gardens. The existence of some herbs is well documented by the Bible, while others are rarely mentioned.

Sometimes the Bible refers to herbs by name (e.g., mustard, Mark 4:31-32). At other times, it alludes to them in general terms (Rom. 14:2).

The Latin word for herb is *herba,* meaning "grass," "green stalks," or "blades." Some herbs grow as annuals and die soon after maturing. These usually multiply by reseeding themselves. Others are perennials, which multiply from the root; after a short period of winter dormancy, they sprout again when the spring rains begin. Psalm 37:2 and Matthew 6:30 mention herbs as symbols of a brief life.

A *spice* is a vegetable substance possessing a sharp taste and aro-

Dates. An important food for the Middle East, dates are eaten fresh or dried; they are also used in making wine. The date palm grows 18 to 24 m. (60 to 80 ft.) tall and lives for over 200 years. It reaches its fruit-bearing peak between its thirtieth and eightieth years.

matic qualities. The Bible sometimes used the Hebrew word for spices in general (*bosem*), which literally refers to the rich fragrance of spices (Exod. 25:6; 1 Kings 10:10). At other times, specific spices are mentioned, as in Exodus 30:23, Song of Solomon 4:14, and Ezekiel 27:19.

Spices were grown in Arabia, India, Persia, Syria, Palestine, and Egypt. There was an extensive commerce in spices between these countries (Gen. 37:25). The people of the ancient world possessed an incredible knowledge of how to use spices and herbs.

These plants were used for many purposes, including medicines, food, flavorings, cosmetics, dyes, disinfectants, and perfumes. Often every part of the plant was used: leaves, branches, bark, blossoms, berries, and roots. Many of these herbs and spices are still in use today.

A. Aloes. The King James Version often uses this word in reference to a large tree, known in Hebrew as *ahalim*. Resin and perfume were made from the *ahalim*.

But the *ahalim* is not the true aloe of the lily family; instead, the Bible species had long lance-shaped leaves. The fragrant substance extracted from the wood of this plant was used to embalm the dead (John 19:39) and for perfume (Psa. 45:8; Prov. 7:17; Song of Sol. 4:14).

The "Lignaloes" to which Israel is compared (Num. 24:6) was probably the true aloe plant (genus *Aloe*). Botanists believe this plant originated in India.

B. Anise. The term *anise* mentioned in Matthew 23:23 is derived from the Greek word *anethon*. It refers either to the dill or to the true anise. Both plants are similar and of the same plant family. Both grow about 91 cm. (3 ft.) high with clusters of yellow flowers. The seeds, leaves, and stem are used for medicine and cooking, and were a part of the ancient temple tithe. (Jesus denounced the Jews of His day for carefully obeying small laws, such as the spice tithe, and forgetting the more important ones.) Anise was cultivated in ancient Egypt and other Mediterranean countries, and still grows there today.

C. Balm or Balsam. The *balm* mentioned in Genesis 37:25 is an extremely fragrant resinous substance extracted from the balsam tree. This was highly esteemed among the ancients (Jer. 46:11).

We do not know whether the balsam tree native to Arabia is the same one mentioned in Jeremiah 8:22 as the "balm of Gilead." The Hebrew word has a variety of spellings—*tzari, sori,* and *tsori;* it literally refers to the fragrance of the plant.

The balsam was a bushy evergreen growing 3.7 to 4.3 m. (12 to 14 ft.) high. The pale yellow gum was used as incense (Exod. 35:28) and dissolved in water as an ointment. The oil obtained from the bark, leaves, and berries was used as medicine. This medicinal "balm" is referred to in Jeremiah 8:22; 51:8 as a symbol of spiritual healing.

D. Baytree or Laurel. The meaning of the *Baytree* in Psalm 37:35 is obscure. The Hebrew word (*ezrah*) means "a green tree in its native soil." The Septuagint, Latin Vulgate, and Revised Standard Version render it "cedar of Lebanon." But the New English Bible translates it to mean "a spreading tree in its native soil."

Henry B. Tristram, author of *Fauna and Flora of Palestine* (1884), theorized that this word refers to the sweet bay tree or laurel. This evergreen is found in northern and western Palestine. It branches from the base, becoming an upright tree with fragrant leaves fitting the Psalmist's description of the "spreading bay tree."

E. Bdellium. This term has two possible meanings:

1. An Aromatic Substance. The Hebrew word (*bedolah*) may refer to a gum resin, similar to balm or myrrh. Genesis 2:12 states that bdellium is a product of the Havilah region in Persia. Numbers 11:7 says that bdellium is the color of manna. Some believe this substance came from a tree that produces a waxy, transparent substance that hardens and resembles pearls.

2. A Mineral. On the other hand, *bdellium* may refer to a mineral; but if so, we do not know which.

F. Bitter Herbs. The people of Israel were commanded to eat the Passover lamb with "bitter herbs" (Exod. 12:8; Num. 9:11) to symbolize their Egyptian bondage. We do not know the kind of herbs or salad that is intended by this Hebrew word (*merorim*, "bitter"). According to the Mishna, these were lettuce, endive, coriander seeds, horehound, tansy, and horseradish. Modern Jews in Egypt and Arabia eat the Passover with lettuce and endive.

G. Calamus. This was a tall reed-like grass with hollow stems. The Hebrew term for this plant (*Keneh bosem*) means "reed of fragrance." It is indeed a very sweet-smelling plant (Song of Sol. 4:14).

The oil extracted from this grass was an ingredient in the anointing oil of Exodus 30:23. The calamus was grown throughout Palestine.

H. Camphire. The only mention of this plant in the Bible is in Song of Solomon 1:14; 4:13. Most scholars consider it to have been the henna. The Hebrew word for the plant is *kopher*.

This shrub grows approximately 3 m. (10 ft.) high. It flourished during Solomon's time at En-gedi and is still growing there today.

The leaves and young twigs were ground into powder and mixed with paste and hot water to produce a reddish-orange dye, which women used to paint their fingernails, toenails, and the soles of their feet. Men also used this cosmetic to paint their beards. The "camphire" also grows in Egypt and other countries in the East today.

I. Cassia. The ingredients of the anointing oil referred to in Exodus 30:24 included the product of the cassia tree. The bark of this tree is similar to cinnamon and is valued for its aromatic qualities.

The spice was available to the Israelites during the Exodus, having perhaps come to them from India by caravan. The Hebrew word for the cassia is *kiddah*. Ezekiel 27:19 implies that the people of Tyre purchased this spice in Dan on the northern border of Palestine.

In Psalm 45:8, the Hebrew word translated as *cassia* is *kesiah*, meaning "fragrant." It seems to be referring to another kind of plant.

J. Cinnamon. A native of Ceylon, cinnamon is a member of the laurel family. The tree grows about 9 m. (30 ft.) high with clusters of yellow and white flowers. Its very fragrant bark yields a golden yellow oil, which was used as one ingredient of the anointing oil (Exod. 30:23) and as perfume (Prov. 7:17).

The Hebrew word for this plant is *kinnamon*. It was one of the chief spices of the ancient Near East.

K. Coriander. The coriander plant belongs to the parsley family. It is an annual that grows 60 to 90 cm. (2 to 3 ft.) high, producing pink or white flowers. When dried, the coriander seeds are pleasant to taste and are used to flavor foods. The Hebrew word for coriander is *gad*.

This plant, known throughout Mediterranean countries from ancient times, was probably introduced to the Israelites in Egypt. When they saw manna in the wilderness, it reminded them of the white seeds of the coriander plant (Exod. 16:31; Num. 11:7).

L. Cummin. This plant is also a member of the parsley family. The Hebrew word for it is *kammon*. Cummin is a low-growing herb with heads of white flowers. When the seeds are dried, they are used for flavoring foods.

Isaiah 28:25, 27 says that, just as the farmer carefully plants his cummin, so God will deal wisely and justly with His people. Jesus used cummin to demonstrate the importance of keeping the whole law (Matt. 23:23).

M. Fitches. Many botanists believe this was the black poppy, commonly known in Palestine. It has fine thin leaves resembling the fennel and is sometimes called the "fennel flower." It grows 30 to 60 cm. (1 to 2 ft.) tall with yellow or blue flowers. Its black aromatic seeds are used for seasoning, and in Bible times they were usually beaten out with a rod (Isa. 28:25, 27).

For the reference to "fitches" in Ezekiel 4:9, see the section on "Rye."

N. Frankincense. Although many types of plants were used as incense, only one is mentioned in Scripture as *frankincense*. The Hebrew word for this plant is *lebonah*, which means "incense" or "freely burning." It is a large, pink-flowering tree, producing a white gum that hardens quickly and is very aromatic when burned. This was used in ceremonial offerings (Exod. 30:34; Lev. 2:1), as an article of luxury (Song of Sol. 3:6), and as a gift for the Christ child (Matt. 2:11).

The "frankincense" tree did not grow in Palestine, but the product was brought there by a caravan (Isa. 60:6; Jer. 6:20).

O. Gall. There are two meanings of the word *gall* in the Bible:

1. A Poisonous Herb. When the Hebrew word *rosh* was translated as *gall*, it was probably designating the hemlock or the opium poppy. Hosea 10:4 says that gall grew wild in the field. (In this passage, the word *rosh* is rendered *hemlock* in the KJV.) Punishment was sometimes likened to gall water (Jer. 8:14; 9:15; 23:15).

2. A Secretion of the Liver. The *gall* mentioned in Job 16:13 and 20:25 represents the Hebrew word *mererah*. It refers to the gall produced by the liver. The "gall of bitterness" in Acts 8:23 probably refers to the same thing. It is a symbol of spiritual enmity to God.

P. Garlic. This plant is known for its strong taste and aroma. It has flat, pointed leaves, and its bulbous root grows in sections called *cloves*.

The Hebrews called the garlic plant *shum*. It is a member of the amaryllis family, closely related to the onion.

Garlic grew abundantly in Egypt and other countries of the Mediterranean. The Israelites cherished memories of eating garlic in Egypt (Num. 11:5), where it was used to flavor breads.

Q. Hyssop. Many different plants may have been the *hyssop* of the Bible. The Hebrew word for this herb is *ezob*.

The common hyssop is a sweet-smelling plant of the mint family. It is a bush growing 30 to 46 cm. (12 to 18 in.) high, with small pointed leaves and spikes of various colored flowers. It was grown in Egypt and Palestine (Exod. 12:22), and was used in the ceremonial rituals of the Israelites (Lev. 14:4, 6; Num. 19:6, 18; Heb. 9:19). Psalm 51:7 refers to the hyssop as a symbol of inner cleansing. First Kings 4:33 shows that Solomon was aware of its vigorous growing habits.

R. Mallow. This spice is mentioned in the Bible only once (Job

---

A Bible Garden

The Bible refers often to gardens, fields, foods, feasts, and eating habits of people. Food was certainly an important aspect of life for the ancients. By cultivating a Bible garden, we can learn much about the eating habits and other customs of Bible times.

Many people find the experience of growing plants mentioned in the Scriptures an exciting way to learn about the Bible lands. This project is well-suited to the home garden, a plot on the church campus, or a small garden space elsewhere.

A Bible garden would include many vegetables that can be grown in the temperate climate of North America, Great Britain, or Western Europe. For example, one could plant beans, lentils, cucumbers, leeks, onions, radishes, and garlic. In warmer climates, a Bible garden could also include melons, grapes, apricots, figs, and pomegranates.

One authority notes that biblical people crushed watermelon and mixed it with water to satisfy their thirst. They mixed juices of fruit with honey to make a tasty fruit punch and dried spring flower petals to brew fragrant teas.

A variety of herbs would also be in a Bible garden. Caraway, cumin, mint, mustard, parsley, sage, and thyme are but a few plants that were used for seasoning food.

Remember that the Israelites observed certain methods of planting that were quite different from our traditional gardening practices. So if you wish to make your Bible garden truly authentic, you may choose to follow these ancient methods.

For example, modern gardeners often plant two crops in the same furrow to take advantage of different growing seasons; but the Israelites could not do this. Seed symbolized the Israelites themselves—the "seed" (descendants) of Abraham— and just as God forbade the Israelites to marry pagan peoples, He forbade them to mix their garden seed (Lev. 19:19; Deut. 22:9). This law constantly reminded the Israelites that they must remain a separate people. God's law also prohibited planting trees near a place of worship (this assured that the Israelites would not revert to pagan tree worship—Deut. 16:21), so gardens near the temple had no fruit trees.

In the dry climate of Palestine, the Israelites customarily planted their crops beside streams (cf. Psa. 1:3; Isa. 19:7), or dug irrigation ditches between the rows of plants (cf. Ezek. 17:7). Our gardens seldom require such special provisions for watering; but you may decide to lay out your Bible garden in this fashion to illustrate the methods that Israelite farmers used. It would also remind you of the symbolic importance of water in the Bible. Isaiah said that when God's people disobeyed Him, they would "be as an oak that fadeth, and as a garden that hath no water" (Isa. 1:30). The writer of Proverbs said that God could direct a king's heart "as the rivers of water: he turneth it whithersoever he will" (Prov. 21:1)— a phrase that reminds us of the irrigation ditches which the Israelites used to channel water wherever they desired. The Bible often cites water as a spiritual symbol, and it was a very familiar commodity for the Hebrew gardener.

The ancients planned, planted, and tended their gardens with care. They enjoyed the fruits of their labor and celebrated the yield with great thanksgiving. We can do the same.

30:4). The Hebrew word for this plant is *malluah* ("salty"); it denotes a plant that has a salty taste or is raised in salty places. The mallow fits this description.

The mallow bush grows abundantly in salt marshes along the Mediterranean and on the shores of the Dead Sea.

It reaches about 3 m. (10 ft.) in height and has tiny purple flowers. Its leaves are eaten by the poor when food is desperately scarce.

S. Mint. The Greek word *heduosmon* is translated *mint* in the New Testament. There are two varieties of wild mint; both grow in Syria and Palestine.

In ancient times, mint was used for medicine and seasoning foods. It may have been one of the "bitter herbs" that the Israelites ate with the Passover lamb. Mint was considered to be one of the least important herbs, even though it was used as a tithe at the temple.

T. Mustard. The black mustard grew wild in Palestine on the shores of Galilee. This herb reached 1.8 to 2.4 m. (6 to 8 ft.) in height and was covered with yellow flowers. The seeds were used to flavor meat and vegetables, and were a favorite food of birds.

Jesus compared the kingdom of heaven to the mustard seed (Matt. 13:31-32; Mark 4:31-32; Luke 13:19). He also used it to teach the power of small faith (Matt. 17:20; Luke 17:6).

Some think the mustard of the Bible was the yellow mustard. But this is not likely, because it is a low-growing plant and not a true herb.

U. Myrrh. The King James Version uses the word *myrrh* with reference to different plants. One of these was a small tree with bushy branches and three-sectioned leaves, bearing a plum-like fruit, and producing a fragrant gum that had many uses. The Hebrew word for this plant was *mor*. It was used in anointing oil (Exod. 30:23), in perfume (Psa. 45:8; Prov. 7:17; Song of Sol. 3:6), and in ceremonial cleansing (Esther 2:12). The magi brought it to the baby Jesus (Matt. 2:11). It was offered to Jesus on the cross (Mark 15:23), and was used to prepare Jesus' body for burial (John 19:39).

The *myrrh* mentioned in Genesis 37:25 and 43:11 was probably the tree *Cistus creticus*. The Hebrew word for this plant is *lot*. This shrub produces pink flowers and is sometimes known as the "rock rose." It is very fragrant and valued for its perfume.

The tree that produces the myrrh used in modern times is not the same genus or species as the myrrh of Bible times.

V. Myrtle. The myrtle tree (Hebrew, *hadas*) of the Bible was probably the common myrtle. Growing 4.6 to 6 m. (15 to 20 ft.) high, it has dark shiny leaves and bears clusters of star-shaped flowers.

The myrtle tree was common to Galilee and northern Palestine and Syria. It also grew around Jerusalem, but was rarer there. Zechariah 1:9-11 mentions that it also grew in the Jordan Valley.

Its branches were used for booths in the Feast of Tabernacles (Neh. 8:15; cf. Lev. 23:40). It reminded the Israelites of God's goodness (Isa. 41:19), by contrast with the brier (Isa. 55:13).

The myrtle was sacred to the ancient Greeks. They used it in their worship of Aphrodite, the goddess of love.

Flowering Almond. The almond tree blooms as early as January in the Holy Land. Ornamental architecture often copied the almond's beauty (Exod. 25:33-34), and Jacob sent almonds to Egypt as a gift (Gen. 43:11).

W. Rue. This important herb is mentioned in the Bible only once (Luke 11:42). The Greek word for it is *peganon*. It is a small shrub with clusters of yellow flowers that have a very strong odor. It is a native to the Mediterranean region, but was cultivated in Palestine as a garden herb. It was used as a disinfectant, medicine, and as the temple tithe.

X. Saffron. The saffron has been cultivated in southern Europe and Asia from very early times. The Hebrew word for it is *karkom*.

The plant, which grows from a bulb, blooms in the fall, with light lavender blossoms, veined red. Their stigmas are dried, pulverized, and pressed into cakes that are used for making yellow dyes, in medicine, and for flavoring. Saffron has a sweet smell but a bitter taste. It is mentioned as one of the common spices of the Old Testament (Song of Sol. 4:14).

Y. Spikenard. This is one of the most precious spices of the Bible. The Hebrew for it is *nerd;* the Greeks called it *nardos*. It grew extensively in northern India, and has been found high in the Himalaya Mountains.

It grows small with many spikes on one root, bearing pink blossoms; thus it is sometimes called the "Indian spike." Perfumed oil is extracted from these spikes.

The New Testament tells how a woman anointed Jesus with this most costly liquid (Mark 14:3-4). According to Werner Keller, "The receptacles for these often expensive items (i.e., perfumes)

Mulberry. The mulberry grows in southern Palestine, and it is still cultivated in Syria for its leaves, on which silkworms feed. Its berries furnished the ancients a tasty drink, which they sweetened with honey and flavored with spices.

have been found by archaeologists under the debris of walls, among the ruins of patrician houses, and in royal palaces."[2]

Z. Stacte. The Hebrew word for this spice is *nataph*, which means "a drop." It is generally believed that this word denotes the gum from the storax tree.

Grown in the region of Galilee, Asia Minor, and Syria, the storax tree reaches up to 6 m. (20 ft.) with dark green leaves. Its clustered white blossoms appear in March. When in bloom, it resembles the orange tree.

The resin of the storax is used as an expectorant. It is mentioned in the Bible only once, as an ingredient for the anointing oil (Exod. 30:34).

FRUITS

The various fruits mentioned in the Bible show not only the fertility of Palestine but the Israelites' ingenuity in growing, harvesting, and preparing them for use. Fruits were eaten fresh, dried, pressed into cakes, and squeezed for juice. Some were used as medicine. According to God's law, all fruit-bearing plants had to be three years old before their fruit could be harvested (Lev. 19:23). Farmers made provision for the poor and widows by leaving some fruit for them.

A. Almonds. The almond has been known since early Bible times (cf. Gen 43:11). The Hebrews called it *shaked*, which means "hasten." This may refer to the fact that the pink blossoms of the almond tree are the first blooms to appear in the spring (Jer. 1:11-12).

Some visitors think that Palestine grows the best almonds in the East. They have been found in the northern regions of Mount Lebanon and Hebron, east of the Jordan, and in Egypt. Under favorable conditions, the tree grows to 6 m. (20 ft.) in height.

Note that when Aaron's rod budded, it brought forth almonds (Num. 17:8).

B. Apples. Different scholars identify the *apple* referred to in Joel 1:12 and the Song of Solomon 2:3, 5; 7:8; 8:5 with apple, quince, and apricot. The Hebrew word used in these passages is *tappuah*.

The ancient Romans prized the apple tree for its fruit. Scholars believe that the Romans introduced them into England. Although our apple tree grows in Palestine today, it is not certain that the Bible refers to it.

Henry B. Tristram and others think that the apple tree of the Bible was actually the apricot (*Prunus armeniaca*), which originated in southern Asia and grows abundantly in the Holy Land. It reaches approximately 9 m. (30 ft.) with very sweet golden fruit. This tree could fit the description of the "apple" in Proverbs 25:11.

C. Figs. The fig tree was cultivated in Palestine and other Mediterranean countries (cf. Deut. 8:8). Although it is not tall, its large leaves and widely spreading branches provide excellent shade. Sitting under a fig tree was typical of peace and prosperity (1 Kings 4:25; Mic. 4:4; Zech. 3:10). The Hebrew word for the fig tree was *teenah*, meaning "to spread out." The Greeks called this tree *syke* and the fruit *sykon*.

There were two crops of figs in ancient Palestine. The early harvest appeared in June and was called the *bikkore* (Hos. 9:10; Isa. 28:4). The later crop ripened continually from August through March; it was called the *kermouse*.

The fig is small and pear-shaped and often forms before the leaves appear. In biblical times, figs were eaten fresh, dried, or pressed into cakes (1 Sam. 25:19; 30:12). Sometimes figs were used as a poultice (2 Kings 20:7). Jesus used a fig tree to teach His disciples the need for spiritual fruitfulness (Matt. 24:32; Luke 13:6).

D. Grapes. The Holy Land has rightly been called "the land of the grapes." Climate and soil conditions in Palestine are well suited for growing grapes.

The Israelites found enormous clusters of grapes growing in Canaan (Num. 13:23). A single grape was reported to be as large as a plum. Since the grapes of Egypt were small, the Israelites naturally were impressed.

Grapes have been the principal agricultural product of Palestine since ancient times. Besides furnishing raisins and wine, the grapes provided juice that was boiled down to the consistency of molasses; the Hebrews called this *debash*, or "honey." This was

Pomegranate. The fruit of this tree provides a refreshing juice that is sometimes used as a base for wine. The pomegranate tree grows 3 to 4 m. (10 to 15 ft.) high and has bright red flowers. Its reddish-maroon fruit is the size of an orange and has many seeds.

probably the "honey" mentioned in Genesis 43:11 and Ezekiel 27:17.

E. Husks. This is thought to be the fruit of the carob tree. The carob is a tall-growing evergreen with clusters of pea-shaped flowers. The fruit appears in large flat pods, 15 to 20 cm. (6 to 8 in.) long. The pods themselves are very sweet, with flat beans inside. Israelite farmers dried the pods and fed them to cattle; humans ate them only in extremity (cf. Luke 15:16).

Tradition says that carob pods were eaten by John the Baptist, and so the fruit is sometimes called "Saint John's bread."

The tree grows wild in Mediterranean countries today. It is related to the North American locust tree.

F. Mulberries. The Hebrew word *baka* ("weeping") is thought to have referred to the mulberry, which grew in southern Palestine. When David fought the Philistines in the Valley of Rephaim, the rustling of the mulberry leaves was his signal to attack (2 Sam. 5:24). Psalm 84:6 refers to the Valley of Baca, which literally meant "valley of mulberries."

New Testament references to the mulberry (Greek, *sykaminos*) denote the black mulberry. In Luke 17:6, most English Bibles translate this word as *sycamine*. The fruit of this tree resembles the blackberry; the leaves are rough and jagged. First Maccabees 6:34

suggests that the juice of these berries was used as a refreshing drink in Palestine.

G. Pistachio Nuts. When Jacob sent gifts to Joseph in Egypt, he included "nuts" (Gen. 43:11). The Hebrew word for this is *botnim*. Most scholars believe this was the pistachio nut. These grow in parts of Palestine, Syria, and southern Europe.

The pistachio tree grows 6 to 9 m. (20 to 30 ft.) high. The oval nuts hanging in clusters resemble the almond; but they are smaller than the almond and very sweet. The Israelites enjoyed eating these nuts just as they came from the tree; they also made them into a confection.

A few scholars believe the word *botnim* refers to the pine nut, walnut, acorn, or some other nut. But these interpretations are not generally accepted.

In describing the "garden of nuts," Song of Solomon 6:11 probably refers to the English walnut. The Hebrew word here is *egoz*. This tree is cultivated in the region of Galilee and along the slopes of Mount Lebanon and of Mount Hermon. Blossoms appear in February and the tree bears fruit in August.

H. Pomegranates. The Hebrew word for pomegranate is *rimmon*. Known in Palestine since earliest times (cf. Num. 13:23), the pomegranate grew wild in western Asia and northern Africa and was cultivated in Palestine.

This sweet-tasting fruit was used in many ways. Its juice was enjoyed as a cooling drink and as wine (Song of Sol. 8:2). Symbols of the fruit were embroidered as decorations around the bottom of the high priest's robe (Exod. 28:33-34) and carved on the pillars of Solomon's Porch at the temple (1 Kings 7:20).

The pomegranate tree grew 3 to 4 m. (10 to 15 ft.) high with bright red flowers. Its reddish-maroon fruit was the size of an orange and had many seeds. The rind contained a large amount of tannin, which today is used as an astringent and in tanning leather.

I. Sycamine. For information on this plant, see the section on "Mulberries."

J. Sycamore Fruit. The Hebrews called this tree *shikmāh*. It belongs to the fig family.

The biblical sycamore grew in Egypt (Psa. 78:47), along the coast of Palestine, and in the Jordan Valley (1 Kings 10:27). Its small yellow fruit is similar to the common fig, it is very sweet and grows in clusters close to the branches. The tree's heart-shaped leaves resemble the mulberry, and so the plant is sometimes called the "fig mulberry." The large spreading branches growing close to the ground provided Zacchaeus an opportunity to get a better view of Jesus (Luke 19:4). Amos gathered the fruit of this tree for a living (Amos 7:14).

WOOD

From earliest times, man has depended on the earth to provide the resources for his survival. Wood was an important source of shelter, fuel, and decoration.

Wood was always available to the people of Israel, and they became skilled in woodcutting. In fact, they were called "hewers of wood" (cf. Deut. 29:11; 17:15-18). The Israelites used wood for four main purposes: fire, worship, shelter, and commerce.

A. Almug; Algum. These English words are just forms of the same Hebrew word. Solomon requested "algum" wood from Leb-

Cedars of Lebanon. Ranging from 21 to 24 m. (70 to 80 ft.) tall, the cedar of Lebanon has long, spreading branches that occasionally grow over 30 m. (97 ft.) across. The ancient Assyrians, Babylonians, and Egyptians used its fine timber, noted for beauty and strength. It was also used in the temple at Jerusalem (1 Kings 7:12). In ancient times, the mountains of Lebanon were covered with these magnificent trees; but after 40 centuries of logging, only a few isolated plantations remain today.

anon (2 Chron. 2:8) and "almug" was sent from Ophir (1 Kings 10:11-12). We are not sure what kind of tree this was, but Bible scholars generally believe that it was sandalwood.

The almug tree was used for making the columns in Solomon's Temple, and for musical instruments. As we have noted, Solomon imported this wood from great distances.

B. Ash. The Bible mentions this tree only once, in Isaiah 44:14. The true ash is not native to Palestine, so the Septuagint translators understood the Hebrew word (*oren*) to mean the fir tree. Jerome took it to mean the pine. The Revised Standard Version translates it *fir*, and puts *ash* in the margin. Some scholars are of the opinion that the Syrian fir is the one mentioned. This tree grew on Mount Lebanon and was used to make idols.

C. Box Tree. The box tree was one of those mentioned as the "glory of Lebanon." It has small glossy foliage and grows about 6 m. (20 ft.) high. The Hebrews called it *teashur*.

The hard, highly polished wood of the box tree was used in Solomon's Temple (Isa. 60:13). Box wood has been used for musical instruments since Roman times.

D. Cedar. The most valuable and majestic trees described in the Bible are the "cedars of Lebanon." The Hebrew word for this tree was *erez*. It grows to a height of 21 to 24 m. (70 to 80 ft.), with long, spreading branches. The branches of one tree were 33.8 m. (111 ft.) across. The trunks of some cedars are 9 to 12 m. (30 to 40 ft.) in circumference. These huge trees continue to grow for hundreds of years. They were symbols of strength and durability, and noted for their toughness (cf. Psa. 92:12; Ezek. 31:3).

The cedar produces 20 cm. (5 in.) cones that take three years to mature. The wood is red and free of knots. Fragrant sap exudes from the trunk and cones (Psa. 104:16; Song of Sol. 4:11). The bitter wood repels insects and resists rot.

The cedar had many uses. Its wood was used for building David's and Solomon's houses (2 Sam. 7:2; 1 Kings 7:12), making idols (Isa. 44:14-15), and constructing ships (Ezek. 27:5).

Cedars grow on Mount Lebanon today; but less than a dozen of these trees stand in the actual groves mentioned by the Bible, near the Lebanon coast of the Mediterranean. All of them have trunks more than 3 m. (10 ft.) in diameter.

The Bible first mentions the cedar tree in Leviticus 14:4. However, some scholars believe this text refers to the juniper, since the Israelites were sojourning in the Sinai Peninsula and the juniper was common in that area. See the section on "Juniper."

E. Chestnut. Most scholars agree that the *chestnut* mentioned in the Bible is the Oriental plane. Jacob's speckled rod was made from the wood of this tree (Gen. 30:37).

Ezekiel mentions the plane tree along with others growing on Mount Lebanon (Ezek. 31:8). The Hebrew word used here is *armon*, meaning "naked" or "bare." This points to the way the bark continually breaks and peels off, exposing the light-colored trunk. The plane tree resembles North America's sycamore or buttonwood trees and will grow to enormous size if left undisturbed. It produces small, spiny balls that hang from the branches. Its leaves are heavily veined, and resemble the maple. It is native to southern Europe, western Asia, and Palestine.

F. Cypress. The Hebrew word *tirza* in Isaiah 44:14 probably refers to the cypress. It is very durable, making it suitable for building, carving, or any fine woodwork. The beautiful red wood of this tree is heavily aromatic. A native of Persia, the cypress was known throughout the Near East and is thought to have grown on Mount Lebanon. Cypress trees were planted in ancient cemeteries, and several mummy cases found in Egypt were made from cypress wood.

G. Ebony. The wood of this tree is mentioned only once in the Bible, when traders from Dedan in Arabia brought it to Tyre (Ezek. 27:15). The Hebrew word for ebony (*hobnim*) literally means "stonewood."

The ebony tree is now found in many Asian countries, as well as India and Ethiopia. It is sometimes 60 cm. (2 ft.) in diameter with a smooth bark; it has white flowers and small edible fruit. Its bark is a whitish gray, but the heart of the wood is black, sometimes streaked with light brown, red, or yellow. Ethiopia is said to have the best ebony wood today.

Highly polished ebony wood was used in Bible times for making musical instruments and ornamental work. The North American persimmon tree belongs to the same genus as the ebony.

H. Fir. Our English Bibles render the Hebrew word *berosh* in a variety of ways to denote different trees of the pine family—especially the fir. The word probably referred only to the Aleppo or

Sipcon pine, which is almost as large as the cedars found on Mount Lebanon. The Aleppo pine was common in Palestine (Hos. 14:8); it was an emblem of nobility (Isa. 41:19-20).

The Aleppo pine has smooth bark, grows up to 8 m. (60 ft.), and produces cones 13 to 15 cm. (5 to 6 in.) long. It was used for making musical instruments (2 Sam. 6:5), floors (1 Kings 6:15), decks of ships (Ezek. 27:5), and houses (Song of Sol. 1:17). Its wood was also used for Solomon's Temple (1 Kings 5:8, 10). Storks built their nests in this tree (Psa. 104:17).

I. Gopher Wood. "Gopher wood" is mentioned only once in the Bible (Gen 6:14). Some scholars believe this is an alternate reading for the Hebrew term *kopher,* which probably means *pitch* or some other resinous material. The Septuagint translates it as *squared wood,* and in the Vulgate it is *planed wood.*

Since cypress trees were used extensively for shipbuilding and grew abundantly in the area, many believe that Noah used cypress wood for the ark. Others have suggested it was the cedar, pine, or fir tree.

J. Oak. English versions translate many different Hebrew words as *oak, terebinth,* or *elm.* They may also translate these words as *place* or *plain.* Some of the Hebrew words are *el, elah, elon,* and *allon.* They generally mean the terebinth or elm trees (Gen. 35:4, 8; Judg. 6:11; 2 Sam. 18:9). The Old Testament often used *oak* to

Seed Cones. The species of cedar that grows on the Lebanon Mountains produces 20 cm. (5 in.) cones that take three years to mature. These cones will produce trees that repel insects and resist rot so well that they will live for hundreds of years.

denote any strong tree or grove. There are 5 species of oak tree in modern Palestine:

Quercus pseudo-coccifera, which has small prickly leaves like the holly. This was Abraham's "oak of Mamre" (Gen. 13:18; 14:13, RSV).

Quercus calliprinos grows large on Mount Tabor and east of the Jordan River. This is believed to have been the "oak of Bashan" (Isa. 2:13; Zech. 11:2).

Quercus aegilops is a deciduous tree that grows in Samaria and Galilee. It does not seem to be mentioned in the Bible.

Quercus sesiliflora grows at high elevations in Lebanon. Such a tree was probably the "oak of Moreh" (Gen. 12:6, RSV).

Quercus coccifera is the type of tree that Rebekah's nurse, Deborah, was buried under. The Bible called that particular tree the "oak of Bethel" or the "oak of tears" (Gen. 35:8).

Though Mount Lebanon was famous for its great cedar trees, Palestine was the land of the oaks. The wood of oak trees was often also used for making idols.

K. Pine. The *pine* of the Old Testament represents the word *tidhar*. Actually the word has two meanings.

1. An Evergreen. *Tidhar* may refer to an evergreen, such as cedar. This fits Isaiah's references to the "pine" that he says grew on Mount Lebanon and was used for Solomon's Temple (Isa. 41:19; 60:13).

2. A Deciduous Tree. *Tidhar* may also refer to the "oil tree," as in Nehemiah 8:15. The Revised Standard Version uses the term "wild olive" in this instance. See the section on "Olive."

L. Shittah or Acacia. The Hebrew word for the acacia tree was *shittah*. Thus the Old Testament often refers to acacia wood as "Shittim wood."

Two species of the acacia are found in Palestine: the *Acacia nilotica* and the *Acacia seyal*. These are quite similar. They grow 4 to 8 m. (15 to 20 ft.) high, with large thorns and hard wood suitable for building. Both have yellow flowers and produce long pods with beans inside.

God instructed the Israelites to build a tabernacle of shittim wood. The tree was probably growing in the region of the Sinai Peninsula, so it was familiar to the Israelites at that time. The Hebrews used shittim wood for boards, altars, pillars, tables, staves, and bars for the tabernacle (Exod. 25:5, 10, 13; 26:15, 26; 27:1; 30:1). Acacia trees grew along the Jordan Valley from the Sea of Galilee to the Dead Sea (Isa. 41:19).

M. Teil. The Hebrew word *elah* is often translated *oak, elm,* or *terebinth.* But in Isaiah 6:13, the King James Version translates it as "teil tree." This is another name for the linden tree, also known as the basswood. This tree does not grow in modern Palestine.

Many scholars believe this passage refers to the terebinth, which grew throughout Palestine. It produced clusters of red berries and may have yielded a form of turpentine. In the Apocrypha, Ecclesiasticus 26:16 gives a poetic description of this tree. Gideon may have met the angel under the wide-spreading branches of a terebinth tree (Judg. 6:11-12).

N. Thyine. Mentioned only in Revelation 18:12, this small, low-growing, coniferous tree belongs to the cypress family. It is native to North Africa and may have been used in the construction of Solomon's Temple. The thyine tree was highly valued by the Romans for cabinetmaking, and its aromatic wood was burned for incense.

ADDITIONAL PLANTS

Some plants mentioned in the Bible were used in a variety of ways. Since these plants served very useful purposes in Bible times, they deserve individual consideration.

A. Bulrushes. Two Hebrew words refer to this plant—*gome* and *agmon.* Sometimes our English versions simply call it the "rush" (cf. Isa. 9:14; 35:7).

Scholars generally believe this plant was the papyrus. It grew abundantly in northern Egypt along the banks of the upper Nile. Although it still grows there today, overuse has made it scarce. It also grows in northern Galilee at the mouth of the Jordan.

Papyrus is a shallow-rooted plant that grows in mire (Job 8:11). It reaches about 3 m. (10 ft.) high on an unbranched stem, which is 5 to 8 cm. (2 to 3 in.) in diameter at the base. A large tufted head at the top of the stem droops when the plant is mature (Isa. 58:5).

The Egyptians used this plant for making boats (Isa. 18:2) and fishing rope (Job 41:2, RSV). They used its sap for sugars, medi-

Terebinth. The terebinth is a spreading tree, usually less than 8 m. (25 ft.) high, which grows in warm, dry, and hilly places in Palestine. It is often considered sacred. This particular tree is part of a small grove surrounding the ruins of a Roman temple at Yajuz in Gilead.

cine, and fuel. The pithy substance inside the stem was eaten. More important for us today is the fact that the Egyptians first manufactured paper from this plant. Many manuscripts on papyrus have helped us learn more about the text of the Bible.

B. Cockles. No one is certain what the *cockle* really was. The Hebrew word *boshah* literally means "stinking like carrion."

The word probably refers to weeds in general, as Job 31:40 seems to imply. Perhaps it refers to weeds with a foul odor, as the Hebrew word suggests.

Some think it denotes the *Arum* genus of marsh plants that grow in Asia today. However, this explanation does not fit the Bible's references to cockles growing "instead of barley" in open fields (Job 31:40).

C. Cotton. The Revised Standard Version renders the Hebrew word *karpas* as *cotton*. It literally means "to be white," so the King James Version often translates it as *fine linen* (Gen. 41:42; 1 Chron. 4:21).

India first cultivated cotton, and subsequent growth of the crop probably spread to Persia (Esther 1:6) and Egypt. Cotton was an important commodity of trade in the ancient world.

D. Flax. Flax was cultivated in Egypt from ancient times (cf. Exod. 9:31). The Hebrew word for this plant was *pishtah*.

Flax grew in fertile soil. It reached about 90 cm. (36 in.) high, with delicate light blue flowers.

Flax was an important crop in Egypt and the rest of the ancient world. To harvest flax, farmers pulled it up by the roots and spread it to dry on housetops. It was customary for women to perform this task, and this chore was considered the mark of a virtuous woman (Prov. 31:13). Hebrew flax was grown in Canaan before the conquest under Joshua. Its woody stems furnished fiber for fine linen (Isa. 19:9; Luke 23:53).

Today, linseed oil is extracted from flax seeds. We do not know whether this was done in Bible times.

E. Grass. Of all the plant kingdom, grass is probably the item most useful to man. Many kinds of grasses are listed in the Bible.

Sometimes the Bible uses *grass* to refer to cereal grains or to herbs in a general way (Isa. 51:12). At other times, Scripture makes a distinction between "grasses" intended for man and those that were food for cattle (Psa. 104:14). Grass was used to symbolize man's brief life on earth (Psa. 90:5; 103:15-16). In teaching His disciples their worth to God, Jesus mentioned the custom of burning dry straw, herbs, and stubble in ovens (Matt. 6:30).

F. Hay. When the word *hay* is mentioned in English versions of the Bible, it does not mean dried grass stored for cattle. Hebrew farmers did not store food for their cattle in this way. Instead, *hay* refers either to green shoots of grass or mown grass (Prov. 27:25; Isa. 15:6).

G. Juniper Bush. This should not be confused with the juniper

Shittah. Also known as the acacia tree, two species of the shittah are found in Palestine, growing between 4 and 8 m. (15 to 20 ft.) high. The wood is commonly used in building. The tabernacle was primarily built of shittah (pl., *shittim*) wood (Exod. 25:10-11;26:15).

tree. This shrub grows about 4 m. (12.1 ft.) high in the sandy soil of the Jordan Valley and along the Sinai Peninsula.

Its twiggy, almost leafless branches bear clusters of pinkish flowers. It is a member of the broom family. The Hebrew word for it is *rothem*.

Desert travelers used this bush for shade. For example, Elijah rested under a juniper bush in the wilderness of Judah as he tried to escape from Jezebel (1 Kings 19:4). Sometimes, in dire situations, the bitter roots of the juniper were eaten (Job 30:4).

Bedouins used the root of the juniper for charcoal, and this may have been done during Old Testament times (Psa. 120:4).

H. Lily. Flowers grew abundantly in Palestine—on hills, in valleys, in gardens, beside water, and in open fields. Yet Scripture mentions the lily more often than any other type of flower.

No particular lily may have been meant by the Song of Solomon (2:1-2; 5:13; 6:2). The Hebrew word for this plant was *shushan*. Arabs use the word *susan* to refer to beautiful flowers in general.

Because of its bright color, abundance, and beauty, the anemone could be the flower referred to in Matthew 6:28-29. Various other kinds of flowers grew in Palestine—such as gladioli, anemones, lilies, hyacinths, tulips, and irises. So it is doubtful whether Jesus had any specific flower in mind when He referred to the "lily" in His Sermon on the Mount.

I. Nettles. The plants that the Bible calls *nettles* were probably thorny weeds growing over neglected or uncultivated land (Prov. 24; Isa. 34:13; Hos. 9:6; Zeph. 2:9). The Hebrew word behind this term is *kimmosh*. Although the term may not refer to a specific plant, it could possibly mean the "Roman nettle." This species is still growing in Palestine today.

J. Olives. The olive tree has been known since very early times (Gen. 8:11). It is generally believed to have come from North India and was flourishing in Canaan before the conquest under Joshua (Deut. 6:11). The olive tree is approximately the size of the American apple tree and produces beautiful clusters of white flowers (cf. Hos. 14:6). The olives are green when immature, then turn black as they ripen.

In autumn, the olives were harvested by beating the branches with a stick. Some were left on the tree for the poor (Deut. 24:20).

Olives were grown chiefly for their oil, which was used in cooking. The oil was also used for fueling lamps, grooming the hair and skin, and for religious rites. Olive wood was used for Solomon's Temple (1 Kings 6:23, 31-33), and olive branches formed booths for feast days (Neh. 8:15).

An olive tree does not bear fruit until its fifteenth year, but it grows for hundreds of years. The "wild olives" mentioned by Paul in Romans 11:17-24 grew on a low bush.

K. Palms. The date palm grows from 18 to 24 m. (60 to 80 ft.) high and lives over 200 years. The Hebrew name for it was *tamar*. The Bible describes it as being "upright" (Jer. 10:5). Indeed, 2 m. (6 ft.) leaves branching from the top give this tree a very tall appearance. The date palm flourished throughout the Near East, especially around the Nile River and the Red Sea. Bethany was called the "house of dates" and Jericho "the city of palm trees."

The palm tree was useful in many ways, most of all because of its fruit. It bears the most fruit between its thirtieth and eightieth years. Dates are eaten fresh or dried, and some are made into wine.

Carvings of palm trees decorated Solomon's Temple (1 Kings 6:29, 32, 35). Palm branches were used to make booths for feast days (Neh. 8:15). The shoots that sprouted around the bottom of the trunk were used for ropes, sandals, and baskets.

In Psalm 92:12, the palm is a symbol of the righteous. Palm branches were spread before Jesus as he entered Jerusalem (John 12:13).

L. Papyrus. See the section on "Bulrushes."

M. Reeds. The *reed* of Egypt and Palestine resembled bamboo; it grew very thick in marshy areas (Job 40:21). Its 4m. (12ft.) stems are hollow and may have been used for musical instruments. The reed has a massive purple bloom at the top that bends in the slightest breeze (Matt. 11:7). Isaiah and Jeremiah refer to it as "cane" (Isa. 43:24; Jer. 6:20). The Hebrew word for it was *kaneh*; the Greeks called it *kalamos*.

The Bible uses cane to symbolize the punishment of Israel (1 Kings 14:15). Cane denoted weakness (2 Kings 18:21; Ezek. 29:6). It also functioned as a unit of measure, because of its uniformly jointed stem (Ezek. 40:3, 5). The Roman soldiers used a reed to ridicule and abuse Jesus (Matt. 27:29-30).

N. Roses. The Hebrew word signifying the true rose (*rhodos*) is only mentioned in the deuterocanonical books of Ecclesiasticus (24:14; 39:13; 50:8) and The Wisdom of Solomon (2:8). However, the maid who recognized Peter at the gate was named *Rhoda*—literally meaning "a rose" (Acts 12:13-16).

It is doubtful whether the Hebrew word *habazeleth* actually means *rose* in Song of Solomon 2:1 and Isaiah 35:1. Some scholars suggest that the "rose of Sharon" was in fact the narcissus, which blooms in the spring on the Plain of Sharon. Others think this term refers to the meadow saffron, with its lilac-colored flowers. Still others think that the "rose of Sharon" was a form of the papyrus, which blooms on Sharon each autumn.

The wild rose is seen only in the extreme northern portions of Palestine, while the true rose is a native of Media and Persia. The true rose was later brought to the countries of the Mediterranean and grows today on the mountains of Palestine.

O. Soapwort. Before the manufacture of soap as we know it today, people in Palestine used a crude form of soap made from the ashes of the roots of the soapwort, mixed with olive oil.

The Hebrew words for these soap plants—*bor* and *borith*—literally meant "that which cleanses." For making soap, the Hebrews used several types of scrubby alkaline plants that grew in the area of the Dead Sea and the Mediterranean. They often used this soft soap for bathing (Job 9:30; Jer. 2:22).

Anemone. The "lily" is the most frequently mentioned flower in the Scriptures. Probably no particular species of flower is meant in most references; but in Christ's description of the lily (Matt. 6:28-29), the flower referred to may well be the anemone. This bright red species grows abundantly throughout Palestine.

Generally, Hebrew women used the root of the soapwort for washing linens, because they believed it would not make them shrink. Men used the ashes of the glasswort and the saltwort to make potash for smelting metals (Isa. 1:25; Mal. 3:2).

P. Straw. After Israelite farmers threshed their grain, they fed the remaining straw to cattle and work animals (Gen. 24:25, 32; Judg. 19:19; Isa. 25:10). During their Egyptian bondage, the Israelites mixed straw with clay to make bricks; this was to prevent the bricks from cracking. When the pharaoh took their straw away, they gathered stubble in the field and chopped it for straw (Exod. 5:7, 12, 16).

Straw was used as a symbol of weakness in Job 41:27.

Q. Tares. The Bible mentions "tares" only in Matthew 13:25-40. The Greek word for this plant is *zizanion*. The seeds are poisonous, producing dizziness and sometimes death if swallowed. The

Olive. Approximately the size of an apple tree, the olive produces beautiful clusters of white flowers. The olive will not produce fruit until its fifteenth year, but will live for hundreds of years. In biblical times olives were grown primarily for their oil, which was used in cooking, fueling lamps, and grooming the hair and skin. The trees shown here are in a garden at Emmaus.

modern name for this plant is the "bearded darnel" (*lolium temulentum*). It is a grass very common in the Near East, and looks very similar to wheat until it begins to head. Darnels are usually left in the field to ripen until harvest, and then are separated when the wheat is winnowed. Since the grain of the "tares" is smaller and lighter than the wheat, it is blown away with the chaff. If any tares remain, they are passed through a sieve and separated from the wheat.

R. Thorns and Thistles. Many Hebrew words denote thorny plants, and are variously translated as *bramble, brier, thorns,* or *thistles*. For example, the Hebrew word *choach* is usually translated *thistle*. Actually, it refers to many kinds of prickly plants (Judg. 8:7, 16).

Probably the most well-known of the thorns of Palestine is called the "crown of thorns." This is a small tree that grows 6 to 9 m. (20 to 30 ft.) tall, whose thorny boughs Roman soldiers plaited for Jesus' head at the Crucifixion (Matt. 27:29).

The shrubby plant called "burnet" grows in Judea, Galilee, and around Mount Carmel. It was used for feed and for fueling the baker's oven (Eccl. 7:6).

Many of these prickly plants cover the land and choke the crops (Matt. 13:7). Modern Israeli farmers sometimes cut them before they go to seed.

Hosea alludes to the way the Israelites fortified their walls by placing thorny branches along the top (Hos. 2:6). The Old Testament often spoke of thorns as symbols of punishment (Num. 33:55; Judg. 2:3; Prov. 22:5).

S. Willows. The Septuagint, the Latin Vulgate, and most English versions have rendered the Hebrew word *aravah* as *willow*. Although several species of willow grew in Palestine, it is generally believed that this word refers to the Babylon willow, which flourished on the banks of the Euphrates (Psa. 137:2; Isa. 44:4).

God instructed the Israelites to build booths for the Feast of Tabernacles out of willow branches (Lev. 23:40). After the captivity in Babylon, the willow became an emblem of sorrow (Psa. 137:1-2).

The true willow has long narrow leaves, hanging on drooping branches. The flowers are small furry catkins that appear before the leaves. The seed pods split open and release furry seeds to the wind. This beautiful tree is rarely seen today in the Holy Land.

Palm. The palm tree flourishes throughout the Near East, and carvings of palm decorated King Solomon's Temple (1 Kings 6:29-35). Palm leaves called "branches" were used to make booths for feast days (Neh. 8:15). They were also woven into baskets, ropes, and sandals.

T. Wormwood. This plant is distinguished for its bitter juice (Lam. 3:15). Several species grew in the arid regions of Palestine and northern Africa.

Scholars believe that wormwood (Hebrew, *laanah*) was either the absinthium, which yielded oil for medicinal purposes, or a low-growing shrub with small leaves and heads of yellow-greenish flowers.

The Bible refers to wormwood—along with gall and hemlock—to signify bitterness (Rev. 8:11). In Deuteronomy 29:18 it symbolizes the disobedient, and in Jeremiah 9:15; 23:15 it is used to denote punishment.

5

AGRICULTURE

Agriculture refers to the various operations connected with the cultivation of the soil. It includes the sowing and harvesting of vegetables, grains, and fruits or flowers, as well as the raising of animal herds. Hebrew agriculture developed with the growth of the Hebrew nation.

THE DEVELOPMENT OF FARMING

Tilling the soil became mankind's first occupation when God put Adam and Eve in the garden "to dress it and keep it" (Gen. 2:15). Adam's son Cain tilled the soil while his other son, Abel, tended sheep (Gen. 4:2). Noah kept the first vineyard (Gen. 9:20).

The patriarchs became skillful herdsmen, and Joseph described his brothers as shepherds. But by the time the Hebrews entered Canaan, they had mastered many other agricultural skills. They had seen the Egyptians using the waters of the Nile for irrigation and cultivating large fields of cotton. However, Moses warned his companions that they would face very different agricultural problems in Canaan: "For the land, whither thou goest in to possess it, is not as the land of Egypt" (Deut. 11:10-11).

Mosaic law encouraged agricultural development among the Hebrew landowners (Deut. 26:1-11). Farming became an honorable career as people of the soil earned a living by the sweat of their brows. When the Hebrews entered the Promised Land, each family received its own allotment of land. The law did not permit a family to sell its land or to relinquish permanent rights to it; it was to remain the family inheritance (Deut. 19:14).

A HOLY PARTNERSHIP

The Hebrew farmer looked upon his land as a gift from God, and he believed that he was to be a faithful steward of it (Deut.

11:8-17). The farmer engaged in many activities that expressed this holy partnership with God.

A. Feasts and Festivals. The Hebrews' religious calendar revolved around the cultivation of crops, and the major fasts and feasts had an agricultural significance, for they marked the seasons of planting and harvesting. These events enhanced the worker's sense of personal worth and enriched his faith in God. The Hebrew farmer worked with God to produce the best crop possible. He usually began the farming season with fasting and concluded it with feasting and worship at the time of harvest (e.g., Deut. 16:13-17).

Each farmer paid one-fifth of his produce to God (Lev. 27:31), just as the Egyptians paid one-fifth of their produce to the pharaoh after Joseph bought all the land during Egypt's drought (Gen. 47:20-26).

Every seventh year was a sabbatical year when Israelite farmers did not plant any crops on their lands. It provided rest for the soil and emphasized the people's dependence upon God, since they depleted their reserves of food during the sabbatical year.

B. Property Protection. Israelite farmers enclosed their gardens and vineyards with hedges or walls (Isa. 5:5). But it was not possible to build walls around large fields. To prevent border disputes in the fields, the law placed severe punishment upon anyone who removed the boundary stones used as land marks (Deut. 27:17). The Romans later considered such stones to be minor deities under the god Terminus.

The Hebrew landowner seldom visited his fields during the growing season. Instead he hired watchmen to stay in crude lounges (also called "towers"—Mark 12:1), where they protected the crop from beasts, birds, and marauders.

CONDITIONS AFFECTING AGRICULTURE

The farmers of Israel found unique challenges in the water and soil of Palestine.

A. Soil. The country's irregular land surface offered a variety of soil, frequently fertile but shallow and rocky (Isa. 5:2). The soil varied from dark, heavy loam to light, well-aerated sand.

The coastal plains provided the most productive area, where even bananas and oranges flourished. The land of the plains supported almost every kind of cultivated fruit and vegetable.

The Lower Jordan Valley provided one of the most naturally fertile growing areas in the world. Its tropical climate produced abundant fruit.

The hill country of Judah offered excellent grazing pastures and natural terraces where the soil had built up behind rock walls. The higher elevations received snow during the winter, providing additional water. The plateau of Perea, east of the Jordan, contained soil from eroded lava beds that made it exceedingly fertile. Decayed limestone enriched the soil around Bashan, making it a vast natural wheat field.

Some areas produced two crops per year because they were so fertile (Amos 7:1). Today, after much soil erosion, the land of Palestine still yields rich crops where water is available.

The Israelite farmer found a variety of weather patterns in his native land. The extreme difference in the rain of the mountains and the drought of the desert, plus the contrast between freezing

Terracing. A series of retaining walls prevents soil erosion in hilly areas of Palestine. Stony ledges often provide natural terraces. Olive trees grow on these man-made terraces at Bethlehem.

cold and tropical heat, allowed the farmer to grow many different crops. Modern visitors may find snow in Jerusalem while open markets only a few kilometers away sell strawberries.

Biblical Palestine was more heavily wooded than Palestine is today; it had more ground cover and orchards than now. Deuteronomy 8:7-8 accurately describes the land as the Hebrews found it. Since that time, overproduction of crops, wartime pillage, and other changes have stripped away much of this ground cover. The modern state of Israel is attempting to restore trees and grass that will hold the vital topsoil.

B. Rainfall Patterns. The pattern of rainfall dictated the way a season would develop. Steady rainfall, coming at critical times, produced better crops than heavy, intermittent rainfall.

The farmer in Palestine had to contend with a five-month rainless summer (May to October); and if the following autumn rains were sporadic, the results could be disastrous (Amos 4:7). Three months without rain during autumn would destroy most crops. The Bible speaks of "early" and "latter" rains (Deut. 11:14). The "early" rains were the first autumn showers and the "latter" rains were the last spring showers. Between these were the rains of January. The "early" rains prepared the soil for the seed and the "latter" rains filled out the crops for harvest. The amount of rain

Drawing Water. This painting from a tomb at Thebes shows an Egyptian gardener drawing water by means of a fulcrum-counterweight device. The painting dates from about the thirteenth century B.C. The Hebrews depended on irrigation less than the Egyptians did.

received in different locations varied greatly. For example, in modern Palestine, Jericho receives 14 cm. (5.5 in.) of rainfall per year while areas in Upper Galilee have gotten 117 cm. (47 in.) per year.

However, the farmers of Israel could not rely solely upon the rainfall. When the dry season arrived they depended upon the dews and mist (Gen. 27:28; Deut. 33:28). A heavy dew comes in late August and September. Even today, dew in the hill country and coastal plains will roll off a tent like an early morning rain. This extra moisture provided daily sustenance through the long dry seasons. The absence of dew was considered a sign of God's disfavor (Hag. 1:10).

Winters were moderately cold but could be severe at night, especially in the highlands. Frost and snow lay upon the mountains until April or May. When the frost and snows of winter departed, harvest came quickly.

Jordan Valley wheat ripened in May. Grain crops on the coastal plains followed in late May, but harvest in higher elevations sometimes waited until late June. Too much moisture during the season would cause mildew and blight, which could destroy various crops (Deut. 28:22; Amos 4:9).

C. Control of Water. The Israelites tried to control their supply of water with wells and irrigation. Shepherds and herdsmen generally provided wells for their flocks, often at great expense (2 Chron. 26:10). A well became a natural center for many social gatherings (Gen. 24:11), a resting place for weary travelers (John 4:6), and the campsite for hungry armies. It was community property. To stop up a well was considered an act of hostility (Gen. 26:15). Tribes frequently clashed over the right to use a well.

A small stone usually covered the well opening. A low stone wall surrounded the well to protect it from blowing sand and to prevent people and animals from falling in.

The farmers of Palestine also depended upon cisterns. They dug these reservoirs underground and cemented them tightly to prevent the water from evaporating. Sometimes farmers carved a cistern out of solid rock, which held the moisture better than a clay-lined cistern. The Nabateans and Romans built dams and reservoirs under their respective governments in the first century B.C. These methods greatly increased the productivity of the land.

The Hebrews practiced irrigation on a much smaller scale than the Egyptians. They used artificial trenches to distribute the water. Irrigation water nourished the large city gardens of Israel. These quadrangular plats were subdivided into smaller squares, bordered by walkways and stone-lined troughs that conveyed water to every plant and tree. Royal palaces were famed for their gardens, which were often used for festivities (Song of Sol. 5:1). There were also public gardens, such as the Garden of Gethsemane.

Palestine's dependence upon the rain made it especially vulnerable to famine. When the rains failed, dry easterly and southerly winds parched the earth. The Bible mentions numerous famines, beginning with Abram's journey to Egypt because of famine (Gen. 12:10). Such droughts could last for several years. Famine was one of the most fearful judgments that God brought upon the land (1 Kings 8:35).

D. Hot Winds. *Siroccos* (hot winds from the eastern desert) worried the farmer from mid-September through October. Siroccos lasted from three days to a week, raising the temperature as much as 20 degrees F. above average. Humidity dropped sharply when the siroccos blew. A prolonged sirocco could spell disaster for the farmer (Isa. 27:8; Ezek. 17:10; Hos. 13:15; Luke 12:55).

E. Insects. Locusts or other insects could destroy a crop. Migratory locusts, traveling in large swarms, can strip all the plant life in their path in a short time. This was always a threat to the Palestinian farmer.

CROP STORAGE

After the harvest, a farmer had to dispose of his produce or store it. He stored most of his crops for his own household, though his harvests often supplied exports (Ezek. 27:17).

Storage places for grain ranged from clay jars to pits in the ground, as large as 7.6 m. (25 ft.) in diameter and nearly as deep. The Hebrews used storage jars to keep their grains, oils, and wines, especially in their homes or shops.

Cisterns and silos stored larger amounts of produce. A circular opening of about 38 cm. (15 in.) made the top easy to seal. Some farmers built their bins under the women's apartments, the most secluded part of their home.

Silos. Fossilized grains of wheat, barley, and lentils were found in these underground silos near Beersheba, dating back to 4000 B.C. The Hebrews stored grain in such pits, some large as 8 m. (25 ft.) in diameter and nearly as deep. They also kept provisions in clay jars that were sunk into smaller pits in their homes.

Jesus described a wealthy man who stored his crops in barns, sometimes called granaries (Luke 12:13-21). The kings of Israel and Judah often built store cities that were filled with such barns.

METHODS OF CULTIVATION

The farmers of Israel raised a great variety of crops and some required special methods of cultivation. (All of the crops mentioned below are discussed more fully in "Plants.")

A. Grapes. Grapes grew plentifully in Palestine and the Hebrews devoted as much time to their vineyards as they did to all other forms of agriculture. The planting, pruning, and cropping of grapevines was hard work that many people considered to be menial (2 Kings 25:12). Yet the hill country of Judah offered grapevines a perfect climate.

To prepare a hillside for planting a vineyard, a farmer had to clear rocks from the ground and build stone hedges to hold the soil. The vines were planted in rows 2.4 to 3.0 m. (8 to 10 ft.) apart. They trailed upon the ground or crept upon stone ridges in search of warm, dry exposure for their fruit, which was sometimes propped up on forked sticks. Trimmed down to permanent stock, the vines were fastened to a stake or trellis, trained upon upright frames, or hung on the side of a house or in a tree.

By forbidding farmers to gather grapes for the first three years (Lev. 19:23), Mosaic Law guaranteed that the vines would be well tended in their formative years. The first pruning came in March. After clusters began to form again, the pruners cut off twigs having no fruit. Again the vine grew new clusters and again the barren branches were pruned.

Once or twice during the growing season, the soil around the vines was dug and cleared of weeds. The vinedressers removed stones and trained the vines upon their trellises.

Wine was squeezed in September, and the Hebrews celebrated this occasion with even more festivity than the harvest (Isa. 16:9). It sometimes resulted in wicked mirth (Judg. 9:27).

B. Grains. Cereal grains were another vital crop of Palestine, and wheat gave the highest yield. We might say the Plain of Esdraelon (Jezreel) was the bread basket of Palestine. The area of Galilee produced the best wheat, but every available valley in the rough West Jordan hill country produced grain. The high Transjordan plateau was also an important grain producer.

Galileans planted fall wheat as the winter rains were beginning, harvesting it between May and June. Farmers in lowland areas like the Jordan Valley harvested their wheat in early May.

The Hebrews harvested abundant barley crops. Since it grew best in the drier climates, they grew much of it in the southeast near the Arabah. Because the climate was too warm to cultivate oats and rye, barley became the Israelites' primary animal feed.

Fitches, spelt, and emmer were inferior grains planted around the border of the fields. They were mixed with wheat or barley to make coarse breads.

C. Olives. The olive touched nearly every phase of Jewish life. Olive wood was used in carpentry and fuel; the olive fruit served as food and olive oil found its way into a variety of medicines and ointments, as well as being fuel for light.

The cultivation of olive trees was routinely simple, requiring only occasional loosening of the soil. Olive trees flourished in the shallow rocky soil of Palestine and required little water. However, the trees could not withstand severe cold, so they found southern Palestine more hospitable than the north.

Olives ripen slowly and the farmer picked them as time permitted. Olives could be eaten after being pickled, but they were valued most for their oil, which was used as a substitute for scarcer animal fats. Farmers extracted the oil in stone presses. They rolled a thick stone wheel over the olives on another flat, circular stone which was grooved to carry the oil to a basin (Mic. 6:15).

D. Dates and Figs. Dates flourished in Palestine, especially in the Jordan Valley north of the Dead Sea. Although the Bible never mentions dates as food, it frequently mentions palm trees so it is logical to assume that the fruit contributed to the diet of the Hebrews. Ancient writers such as Pliny, Strabo, and Josephus wrote of the syrup made from dates. The Mishna refers to date honey and the Talmud mentions date wine. Dates were pressed into cakes, as were figs.

Cultivated from very early times, figs grew on low trees with thick-spreading branches. The pear-shaped fruit of the green fig appeared before the leaves. When the leaves attained some size, their interiors filled with small white flowers. If the leaves came out and no fruit appeared among them, the tree would remain barren for the season (Matt. 21:19).

Figs could be gathered as early as June but the main crop ripened about August; this main crop was the green fig (Song of Sol. 2:13). Figs came from the tree ready to eat, but could be dried and made into cakes.

E. Flax. The Hebrews made linen cloth and rope from flax

(Judg. 15:14; Hos. 2:5, 9), which they harvested in March and April. Farmers used their hoes to chop off the stalks at the ground so that none of the valuable plant would be lost. After the flax was cut, it was laid out to dry in the sun (Josh. 2:6).

F. Other Crops. Lentils, coarse beans, and chick peas were also grown in Palestine. Cucumbers, onions, leeks, and garlic were other plants on the menu of the Israelites.

AGRICULTURAL TOOLS

The Hebrew farmer had only primitive tools. This made his work even more difficult.

A. Plows and Harrows. The plow of biblical times was little more than a forked stick with a pointed end. Handles added control. In patriarchal times the farmers added a copper point to the plow; later, bronze improved on that. Later still, after the tenth century B.C., the iron plow penetrated the soil to a depth of about 12 cm. (5 in.).

Plows were pulled by oxen, camels, or asses, but never by more than a pair of animals. The plow demanded the farmer's constant attention to keep it in the ground; only a careless man would look away. Jesus used this as an example of one not fit to enter the kingdom of God (cf. Luke 9:62).

Once the early rains came ground could be broken. The farmer tilled the hard-to-reach places with a mattock, a broad-bladed pickax, or a hoe. Sometimes a farmer would plow his field twice, crisscrossing directions.

Harrowing broke up the clods after the plowing. Early harrows may have been no more than a wooden plank or log, weighted with stones. Sometimes the farmer rode on the harrow.

B. Sickles. Farmers mowed their fields with hand sickles (cf. Deut. 16:9). The ancient sickle resembled the sickles still used in the Near East; Egyptian monuments show how they looked. Until the early tenth century B.C., the cutting blade of the sickle was made of flint; after that time, it was made of iron.

Workers who reaped grain with a sickle would cut it near the ear, leaving the stubble to be pulled up and used for straw. The grain ears were then carried away in baskets. Sometimes the entire stalk was cut close to the ground and the stalks were bound into sheaves (Gen. 37:7). Then workers removed the sheaves by cart, stacked them, or stored them.

C. Winnowing and Threshing Tools. Grain was threshed and then winnowed by throwing it against the wind, which blew away the chaff. Farmers still use this method in much of the Near East.

Ancient threshing places were high, flat summits 15 to 30 m. (50 to 100 ft.) in diameter and open to the winds on every side. Each

---

The Kibbutz

Kibbutz (key-boots) is an Israeli name for any settlement that is operated on a collective system. Most kibbutzim (plural) in Israel today are agricultural.

The first kibbutz was founded in 1904 by Aaron David Gordon, an immigrant from Russia, on a malaria-infested marshland near the southwestern tip of the Sea of Galilee. Gordon and others had arrived in Palestine with a dream to "repossess a land," but had little resources.

Pooling what they had, the immigrants purchased the land from absentee Persian owners who referred to it as the "Death Spot" because of the great toll of life it had already taken. The group constructed simple dwellings, built a communal dining room, moved tons of rock by hand, and drained swamps. Almost anyone joining the commune was made part of the whole, with no one owning anything personally. Known today as Degania, the settlement is the showpiece of the kibbutz movement, with attractive and substantial homes and communal buildings, blooming orchards, citrus groves, and flower beds.

Not long after Gordon's arrival, hundreds of thousands of Jews migrated to Palestine, fleeing from the growing political unrest and persecutions of Europe. Most immigrants had little or no possessions with them. To survive they followed the example of Degania *kibbutzniks* (kib-butz dwellers) in setting up communal property.

It is not unusual to find a kibbutz in which (aside from small personal possessions) no one owns anything at all, not even clothes. Community wardrobes, community toys, community books, community tools—even cots are not personally owned. Although mostly modest (some have neither electricity nor running water) a few *kibbutzim* (plural) have prospered to the point of having their own schools, cultural events, small factories, and even swimming pools.

A kibbutz has an executive committee, whose major decisions are subject to the approval of all members. A work committee assigns jobs, and meals are eaten in a communal dining room. Children live in a "children's home," frequently the best building on the kibbutz.

In biblical times, a Jew owned a plot of ground and passed it on to succeeding elder sons. Although early Hebrews lived together for safety and water supply, the family tenaciously held to its individual property. Such ownership of property has been retained in *moshavim* (communities of individual owners), where each member lives in his own house and farms his own land. But members of *moshavim* buy or rent heavy equipment and sell produce. The *moshav* parallels the small village of biblical days.

Winnowing Wheat. In the Near East, sheaves of wheat are still beaten with sticks and trampled by animals to separate wheat grains from the straw. After threshing, the grain is thrown up into the air so that the chaff blows away, in a process known as *winnowing*. Afterwards the grain is passed through a sieve to remove dirt. It is then ready to be ground into flour.

year farmers would level and roll the dirt to keep the threshing floor hard. Often a village had only one threshing floor and each farmer took his turn in a fixed order.

The sheaves were piled in a heap and the grain was beaten out by a machine or by the trampling of oxen's feet. The threshing machine was a square wooden frame holding two or more wooden rollers. On each roller were three or four iron rings, notched like sawteeth. Oxen pulled the machine, and the driver sat on a crosspiece fastened into the frame. As the rollers passed over the grain, it was crushed out on every side and the straw was shredded for fodder. The threshing machine was a symbol of violence and destruction (cf. Amos 1:3).

Another threshing tool was a wooden plank 90 cm. (3 ft.) wide and 2 to 3 m. (6 to 8 ft.) long. On the lower side were many holes 2.5 to 5 cm. (1 to 2 in.) in diameter, where the farmer fastened pieces of stone, flint, or iron that projected from the board as teeth, tearing the grain loose. Unmuzzled oxen pulled the board behind them across the threshing floor, with the driver standing on the plank.

The grain and chaff gradually formed a big heap at the center of the floor. During the days of threshing, the owner slept nearby to protect the grain from thieves (cf. Ruth 3:2-14).

Farmers winnowed their grain with a fan, which was a semi-oval frame about 90 cm. (3 ft.) in diameter with a surface of woven hair or palm leaves. A worker would hold the fan by hand while others poured the mixture of grain and chaff upon it. Then the winnower tossed the grain to the winds so the chaff would be blown away and the heavier kernels would fall to the ground (Psa. 1:4). Winnowing was done in the evening, when sea breezes blew the strongest.

D. Sieves. The first winnowing process did not remove all the unwanted material, so a final step—sifting—was necessary. Amos 9:9 and Isaiah 30:28 describe two kinds of sieves, the *kebarah* in Amos and the *naphah* in Isaiah. We are not sure which type of sieve is meant in either passage. One type of sieve now used in the Near East has a fine mesh that retains the good grain and lets the dust pass through. Another kind, with coarse mesh, allows the desired grain to fall through and retains the larger husks and pods, either to be thrown out or to be rethreshed.

E. Mills and Presses. Corn and other grains were ground with mortar stones. One or two persons in a household ground grain daily for the family's meals.

Vinedressers cut grapes from the vine with sickles and carried them in baskets to a winepress. This was usually a large stone vat with a small channel that allowed the grape juice to pour out the side into a tub. The grapes were trodden by foot, then pressed by machine. Farmers stored the grape juice in skin bottles, pitchers, and barrels, where it fermented into wine. They also obtained olive oil with presses.

AGRICULTURAL SYMBOLS

The Bible abounds with agricultural symbolism. For example, we read that a blessed man is one whose life is watered by God's Spirit as an irrigation stream waters a fruit tree (Psa. 1). God's favor comes like the dew on the grass (Prov. 19:12). An evil man is sifted like chaff (Psa. 1:4). Men faint for God while living in life's dry barren deserts (Psa. 63:1). And forsaking God is like living with a leaky cistern (Jer. 2:13).

Jesus often used agricultural symbols in His teaching. He described a sower scattering his seed (Mark 4:1-20) and laborers who answered a call to work in a vineyard (Matt. 20:1-16). He compared false prophets to trees that bear bad fruit (Matt. 7:15-20) and warned that "every tree is known by his own fruit" (Luke 6:43-44). Jesus promised to give His followers "living water" from everlasting wells (John 4). He used seeds, vines, trees, fruit, and other agricultural metaphors to express the truths of God.

The early Christian writers also used the common knowledge of agriculture to convey their message. For example, Paul recalled the unmuzzled ox at the threshing floor when he asked churches to support their spiritual reapers (1 Cor. 9:10). John described the angel of judgment thrusting in his sickle, "for the harvest of the earth is ripe" (Rev. 14:15). Seldom was a preacher or writer better understood than when he used the simple things of nature to illustrate his message.

FOOTNOTES

Chapter Three: "Animals and Insects of Palestine"

[1]A. H. Brodrick, *Animals in Archaeology* (New York: Praeger Publishers, 1972), p. 49.

[2]Walter Ferguson, *Living Animals of the Bible* (New York: Charles Scribner's Sons, n.d.), p. 37.

[3]Peter Farb, *Land, Wildlife, and Peoples of the Bible* (New York: Harper and Row, 1967), pp. 85-86.

Chapter Four: "Plants and Herbs of Palestine"

[1]*Adam Clarke's Commentary*, Vol. 1 (New York: Abingdon Press, n.d.), p. 557.

[2]Werner Keller, *The Bible as History* (New York: William Morrow and Company, 1964), p. 215.

ACKNOWLEDGMENTS

The Publisher gratefully acknowledges the cooperation of the following sources, whose illustrations appear in this book:

American Baptist Association, 66.
Baker Book House, 128, 131, 140, 143.
Denis Baly, 19, 45, 51, 127, 139.
Brooklyn Museum, 97.
Elsevier Publishing Projects, 12.
Episcopal Home, Matson Photo Service, 8, 11, 21, 23, 37, 111.
Ewing Galloway, 103.
Foreign Mission Board, 28, 29, 48.
L. H. Grollenberg, 25, 133.
Iraq Museum, 61.
Israel Department of Antiquities and Museum, 39, 65, 75.
Israel Government Press Office, 22, 43.
Israel Information Service, 153.
Jeep Express, 34.
Levant Photo Service, 47, 117, 144.
The Louvre, 92.
Metropolitan Museum of Art, 150.
Oriental Institute, 86.
Palestine Exploration Fund, 83.
Amikam Shoob, 95, 109.
Standard Publishing Company, 106.
The Times of London, 3.
William Van de Poll, 38.
Howard Vos, 59.
William White, 31, 44, 107, 120, 136, 146, 149.

The Publisher has attempted to observe the legal requirements with respect to the rights of the suppliers of photographic materials. Nevertheless, persons who have claims are invited to apply to the Publisher.

INDEX

This index is designed as a guide to proper names and other significant topics, found in *The Land of the Bible*. Page numbers in italics indicate pages where a related illustration or sidebar appears. Headings in italics indicate the title of a book or some other important work of literature. Use the index to find related information in various articles.